THE
ERM
EXPLAINED

THE
ERM
EXPLAINED

A Straightforward Guide to the
Exchange Rate Mechanism
and the European Currency Debate

Robert Minikin

KOGAN
PAGE

First published in 1993

Kogan Page Limited
120 Pentonville Road
London N1 9JN

British Library Cataloguing in Publication Data
A CIP record for this book is available from the British Library.

ISBN 0 7494 0939 8

Typeset by J&L Composition Ltd, Filey, North Yorkshire
Printed and bound in Great Britain by Clays Ltd, St Ives plc

CONTENTS

• •

ACKNOWLEDGEMENTS

With the ERM evolving rapidly during the preparation of this book, I have drawn heavily on the help of friends and colleagues. My greatest debt is to Kay Sinden and Stephen Childs who influenced the overall approach and gave invaluable assistance at each stage of the book's development. Kay Sinden, along with Ian Amstad, also reviewed the final manuscript — both making very constructive comments. Stuart Trow played an important role in contributing insights into the latest market and policy developments as the book progressed. Of my London Business School MBA year, Ken Charman, Tim Cross and Tom Turcan all provided a steady stream of encouragement and new ideas. Finally, thanks to MCM for allowing me the time to complete the work during a period of exceptional financial market volatility.

INTRODUCTION

The currency turbulence which engulfed the Exchange Rate
Mechanism in September 1992 has reopened the debate on the
workings of the Mechanism and the broader issue of European
monetary union. The Maastricht Treaty can no longer be
seen as the final word on the European single currency, nor on
the steps required to achieve that goal. A Community study has
been launched into the causes of the ERM crisis and may bring
major reforms before sterling and the lira rejoin. But this
controversy does not just involve politicians and central bankers;
businesses are being directly affected by day to day interest rate
and currency gyrations. Citizens across Europe are being asked
to judge the merits of the Maastricht Treaty and decide what
value they put on a national currency. This book sets out
to explain the issues at stake in the ERM debate in non-
technical terms and undertake an impartial review of the
evidence.

How exactly the ERM operates, and why the Maastricht
Treaty's attempt to build on the ERM's success in the 1980s
created the conditions for a currency crisis is the focus of Part I.

In Part II we consider what we should expect to gain by
adopting a single currency and at what cost in reduced national
flexibility and policy independence.

Part III examines the impact of developments in Eastern
Europe on the outlook for a single currency. It also looks at the
question of how the poorer EC regions will fare in a single
currency area, and whether new EC members such as Austria
should be on the fast-track to monetary union.

Finally, we look forward to the prospects for European
exchange rate management over the next five to ten years. There
are no compelling economic arguments that *all* Community
countries should be required to ultimately adopt the ECU in
place of national currencies. Indeed, a core group of Community
countries are better placed to take the first steps in monetary

union. Given this, the prospect for a multi-tier currency system in Europe is considered, a system in which the different and equally valid economic interests of individual nations can be better accommodated.

Part
ONE

•••

THE ERM: ITS STRUCTURE
AND FAULT LINES

•••

HOW THE EXCHANGE RATE MECHANISM OPERATES

•••

BACKGROUND TO THE ERM

The early steps toward a unified Europe were made against the backdrop of a relatively stable international economic order. The United States retained its status as the pre-eminent Western economic power and all European currencies were fixed to the American dollar. The European Economic Community (EEC) was established in 1958 with the initial objective of removing barriers to trade rather than usurping the dollar's international role. Throughout the 1960s, however, plans for greater European integration were advanced, culminating in the 1970 Werner Report. This report explicitly referred to the broader ambitions of economic and monetary union, including the irrevocable fixing of European exchange rates.

These aspirations were given immediate relevance with the breakdown of the dollar-based currency system. With freely floating exchange rates proving exceptionally volatile, a system for stabilising EC exchange rates was put in place. Prior to the establishment of the European Monetary System (EMS) in 1979, there was a pronounced contrast between progress toward economic integration and toward exchange rate stability. The EEC was in a phase of expansion, with the addition of Denmark, Ireland and the United Kingdom to the original Group of Six, but at the same time European countries were increasingly being forced to allow their currencies to float freely.

It was against this backdrop that the inter-governmental European Council decided in mid-1978 to reform the EC approach to exchange rate management and create a 'zone of monetary stability in Europe'. The European Monetary System was born — a system of arrangements to co-ordinate and enhance the effectiveness of currency market management. By March 1979, eight EC currencies (including the Luxembourg franc) were trading according to rules dictated by the new Exchange Rate Mechanism (ERM).

In this chapter, the following aspects of the EMS will be discussed:

- How the Exchange Rate Mechanism contains currency fluctuations.
- The market for foreign exchange: who needs convincing the system will hold?
- The expansion phase of the ERM: before the Maastricht Treaty.
- How the authorities manage the currency markets: the European arrangements for policy co-ordination.

The ECU — a currency for Europe

In the beginning (December 1978), when all around was without form and void, the European Council met and created an ECU. The European Currency Unit is a basket of fixed quantities of EC currencies — it includes 1⅓ French francs, ⅔ of a Deutschmark and so on. These amounts are reviewed every five years and the current quantities, set in September 1989, are listed in Appendix 1. Following the review, the importance of each currency in the ECU's total value should roughly reflect the significance of its economy within the Community. From Figure 1.1 it can be seen that together the Deutschmark and the French franc elements account for half its total value, but all the EC currencies are included right down to the Greek drachma at 0.5 per cent of the ECU. To find out how much the ECU is worth against another currency — say the dollar — we would have to find the value of each of its components and add them together. On 1 May 1992, the ECU buys $1.24. On the same day the pound buys $1.78, so as a rough guide the ECU is worth 70p in sterling terms. Note that we have made no reference to 'the ERM' in this calculation; the ECU's value could still be derived even if 'the ERM' were to disintegrate. Eventually, the ECU may exist in its own right with physical notes and coins, but for the moment, its most important use is as a reference value for the European authorities and financial markets. Transactions between the European central banks can be made in 'official ECUs'. In the private sector, companies use it as the basis for borrowings or loans, while some even write contracts based on its value. One advantage of the ECU as the basis for contracts is that its international value has often been more stable than any single European currency — when the dollar falls sharply against the DMark, in particular, the move may be less pronounced against the ECU. There is no ECU central bank or economic policy and the level of ECU interest rates is almost entirely determined by the average of national interest rates.

'THE ERM' FRAMEWORK FOR CURRENCIES

Having created the ECU, the European central bankers then set about outlining the new system for linking exchange rates together. In previous attempts to do this the value of currencies were fixed against something external — for many years against the value of gold, and more recently against the US dollar. This time they decided to link up all the different currencies *with each other*. How does this work?

Once the EC central bankers and finance ministers have reached agreement on the level at which the currencies should be linked up, they announce central or 'parity' rates for each national currency in terms of the ECU. From this cross rates for all the European currencies can be calculated. As a hypothetical example, let's suppose that they announce the ECU buys two Deutschmarks, or eight French francs or 1,500 Italian lira. Through simple division we can calculate that a Deutschmark is worth four times as much as a French franc, and buys

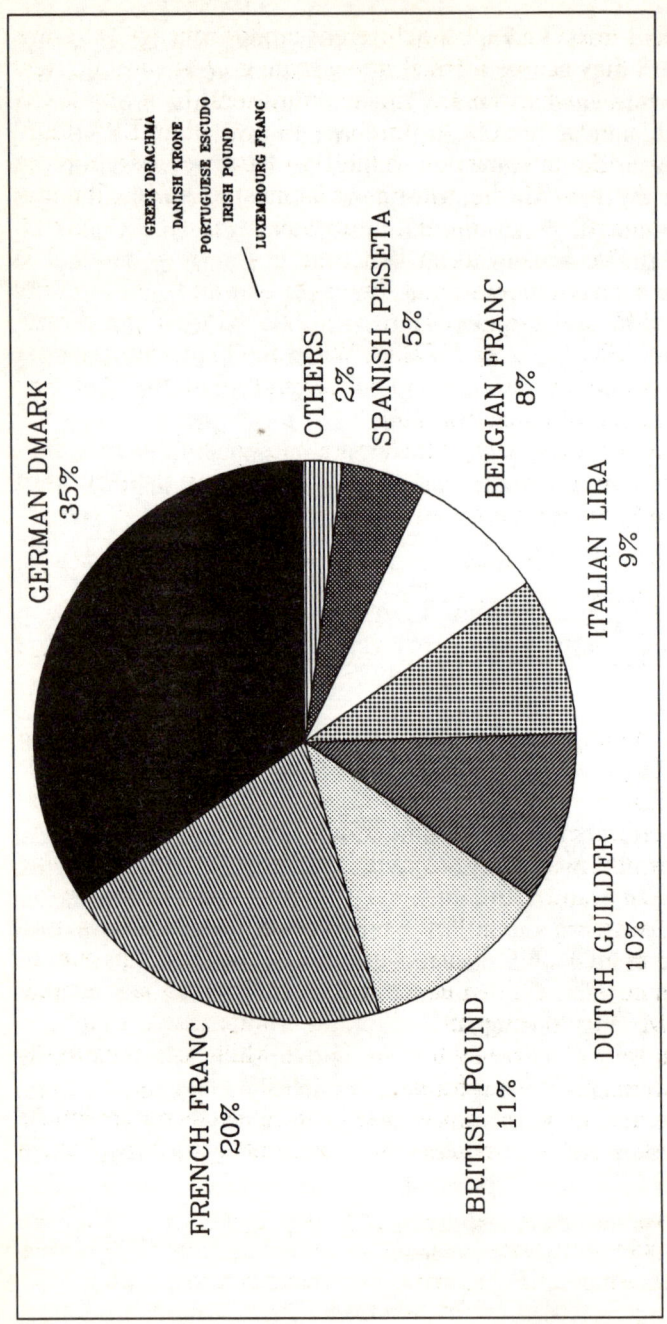

Figure 1.1 Currencies and the ECU — % of total value, September 1992

750 Italian lira. Once all the different cross exchange rates are calculated they can be formed into a large grid of central rates. We now know what the EC finance ministers think any ERM currency should be able to purchase of any other ERM currency. After the introduction of the Portuguese escudo into the ERM in April 1992, the grid was at its most extensive, limiting the movement of all the EC currencies except the Greek drachma. The framework at that time is shown in Table 1.1, with the central rates in bold. The French franc's ECU parity was 6.89509 and the Deutschmark's 2.05586, giving a central rate in the ERM grid of 3.35386. When the Deutschmark buys 3.35386 French francs (circled on the grid), then the DM/FFr rate is trading at its central rate.

Having determined what the central rates should be they then allow the currency markets some say by defining ranges within which any particular cross rate can trade:

- If one of the currencies involved was the Portuguese escudo, the Spanish peseta or the British pound the range was +/−6 per cent.
- For other currencies the range at the time was +/−2.25 per cent.

The recent newcomers to the system had their currencies within a wider range to give their authorities greater flexibility. It was hoped that as their economies became similar to the more established members, and market confidence in their membership grew, the wide ranges would eventually be narrowed. The French franc and the Deutschmark both have narrow ranges, so the Deutschmark can buy no more than 3.4305 francs, and no fewer than 3.2792 francs. When the cross rate hits one of these boundaries the two countries are obliged to take action. With DM/FFr trading at 3.436, the Bundesbank would be forced to sell its currency to buy francs, while the Banque de France would be buying francs for marks.*

There are limits for *each* of the cross rates, and thus before the Deutschmark ever reaches its upper limit against the French

* Note that the limits are not exactly +/−2¼ per cent. They are calculated by multiplying (dividing) the central rate by 1.022753, thus making the entire grid consistent. The exact percentages are +2.275 per cent and −2.225 per cent as a result.

Table 1.1 Bilateral central rates and selling and buying rates in the EMS exchange rate mechanism in the weeks following 6 April 1992

		100 Bfr/Lfr	100 Dkr	100 Ffr	1 DM	I£1	1000 Itl	100 NLG	100 PTE	100 Esp	£1
BF/Ffr	S	–	553.000	628.970	21.0950	56.5115	28.1930	1872.15	25.1900	33.6930	64.6050
	C	–	540.723	614.977	20.6255	55.2545	27.5661	1830.54	23.7241	31.7316	60.8451
	B	–	528.700	601.295	20.1655	54.0250	26.9530	1789.85	22.3435	29.8850	57.3035
Dkr	S	18.9143	–	116.320	3.90160	10.4511	5.21400	346.240	4.65860	6.23100	11.9479
	C	18.4938	–	113.732	3.81443	10.2186	5.09803	338.537	4.38747	5.86837	11.2526
	B	18.0831	–	111.200	3.73000	9.9913	4.98500	331.020	4.13210	5.52600	10.5976
Ffr	S	16.6310	89.9250	–	3.43050	9.18900	4.58450	304.440	4.09610	5.47850	10.50550
	C	16.2608	87.9257	–	3.35386	8.98480	4.48247	297.661	3.85772	5.15981	9.89389
	B	15.8990	85.9700	–	3.27920	8.78500	4.38300	291.040	3.63320	4.85950	9.31800
DM	S	4.95900	26.8100	30.4950	–	2.74000	1.36700	90.7700	1.22100	1.63300	3.13200
	C	4.84837	26.2162	29.8164	–	2.67894	1.33651	88.7526	1.15023	1.53847	2.95000
	B	4.74000	25.6300	29.1500	–	2.61900	1.30650	86.7800	1.08300	1.44900	2.77800
I£	S	1.85100	10.00870	11.3830	0.381825	–	0.510246	33.8868	0.455895	0.609772	1.16920
	C	1.80981	9.78604	11.1299	0.373281	–	0.498895	33.1293	0.429360	0.574281	1.10118
	B	1.76950	9.56830	10.8825	0.364964	–	0.487799	32.3939	0.404371	0.540856	1.03710

Itl	S 3710.20	20062.0	22817.0	765.400	2050.03	—	67912.0	913.800	1222.30	2343.62
	C 3627.64	19615.4	22309.2	748.217	2004.43	—	66405.3	860.626	1151.11	2207.25
	B 3546.90	19179.0	21813.0	731.570	1959.84	—	64928.0	810.500	1084.10	2078.79
NLG	S 5.58700	30.2100	34.3600	1.152350	3.08700	1.54000	—	1.37600	1.84050	3.52950
	C 5.46286	29.5389	33.5953	1.126730	3.01848	1.50590	—	1.29601	1.73345	3.32389
	B 5.34150	28.8825	32.8475	1.101675	2.95100	1.47250	—	1.22100	1.63250	3.13050
PTE	S 447.560	2420.10	2752.40	92.3360	247.299	123.380	8190.00	—	142.020	272.320
	C 421.513	2279.22	2592.21	86.9393	232.905	116.194	7715.97	—	133.753	256.470
	B 396.980	2146.60	2441.30	81.9000	219.350	109.430	7267.00	—	125.970	241.545
ESP	S 334.619	1809.40	2057.80	69.0170	184.892	92.2400	6125.30	79.3850	—	203.600
	C 315.143	1704.05	1938.06	65.0000	174.131	86.8726	5768.83	74.7649	—	191.750
	B 296.802	1604.90	1825.30	61.2170	163.997	81.8200	5433.10	70.4130	—	180.590
£	S 1.74510	9.43610	10.7320	0.359970	0.964240	0.481050	31.9450	0.414000	0.553740	—
	C 1.64352	8.88687	10.1073	0.338984	0.908116	0.453053	30.0853	0.389909	0.521514	—
	B 1.54790	8.36970	9.5190	0.319260	0.855260	0.426690	28.3340	0.367220	0.491160	—
ECU mid-rate	42.4032	7.84195	6.89509	2.05586	0.767417	1538.24	2.31643	178.74	133.631	0.696904

S = Exchange rate at which the central bank of the country in the left hand column will sell the currency identified in the row at the top of the table

C = Bilateral exchange rate

B = Exchange rate at which the central bank of the country in the left hand column will buy the currency identified in the row at the top of the table

Table 1.2 EMS currency rates

Currency	% spread versus weakest currency
Spanish peseta	5.07
Portuguese escudo	4.97
Belgian franc	1.69
Dutch guilder	1.63
Deutschmark	1.42
Irish punt	1.08
Italian lira	0.98
French franc	0.86
Sterling	0.79
Danish krone	0.00

Source: *Financial Times*, 1 May 1992

franc, its appreciation may be constrained by some other currency. If sterling is exceptionally weak, then perhaps this will be the constraint on the Deutschmark's appreciation. Newspapers often quote Table 1.2 which simplifies the matter of watching all the different bilateral exchange rates and highlights the strains in the system.

On 1 May 1992 the Danish krone is the weakest currency — it buys less than its central rates for all the other currencies — while the Spanish peseta is the strongest. This is the point of greatest pressure within the system. Time for a Danish rate increase, or resignation of the government? No: being the weakest currency in the ERM is not by itself a problem and a currency can sit in this position for many months. The table tells us the extent to which the Portuguese escudo is above its krone central rate, 5.07 per cent, and as there is a 6 per cent range for this cross rate, no intervention is required. Note that no single national currency is at the centre of the ERM system. This is in contrast to the system of fixed exchange rates in the 1950s and 1960s which was based on the dollar. It is also designed to be symmetric — when a cross rate hits a limit, action by the central bank of the stronger currency is required, as well as that by the weaker currency's central bank.

The 'ERM grid' has become the focus for management of European exchange rate fluctuations. Intervention at the limits is *mandatory*.* However, let us picture a situation where the Bundesbank suddenly tightens its interest rates while those throughout the rest of Europe are eased. The Deutschmark would appreciate against all the ERM currencies and, even if the DMark failed to hit any bilateral limits, its currency and policies are out of line. As the value of the ECU is simply a weighted average of the national currencies, the DMark would also jump sharply against the ECU. The European Monetary System includes a 'divergence indicator' which reflects a currency's performance relative to the ECU. Its calculation is rather complicated and it is expressed as a percentage of the total possible movement against the ECU given the ERM limits on cross rates. When this indicator hits plus or minus 75 per cent, there is some obligation for the central bank involved to bring its currency closer to the crowd. On 1 May 1992, the peseta's indicator is at 62, and the krone's at −56; not only are no currencies at their bilateral limits but we can also say that none are dangerously 'out of line' with the rest of the system.

MARKET CONFIDENCE IN THE MECHANISM

The role of the currency markets

The foreign exchange markets which the European governments set out to manage dwarf markets for other goods and services. Daily turnover is $470 billion, and of this total London accounts for $300 billion. On an average day, trading on London's currency markets is more than half of the UK's *annual* national output. At times of currency crises, the speculative flows unleashed across London's 400 trading floors appears to dominate even the central banks with their substantial reserves and unlimited short-term credit lines. Trading in the other European financial centres adds to these speculative pressures.

There are two contrasting views of the role of the currency markets. From one perspective the currency markets are simply the messenger. Exchange rates are determined by the relative economic fundamentals in two countries. Excessively rapid

* This requirement only holds during the European day.

money supply growth, or an uncompetitive export sector, point to a lower exchange rate. The currency markets recognise this and rapidly mark the currency down to the appropriate fundamental level. From another perspective, the currency dealers are a source of dangerous instability. The major banks and security houses involved in the market can take positions (net long or short) of a currency running into billions of dollars. They concentrate on making money from unnecessary short-term volatility in the currency markets.

The truth probably lies somewhere between the two extremes. The economic backdrop does influence a currency's true value, but there is considerable uncertainty as to what this true value is. It is rather like asking people passing your front door how much your house is worth. There will be a range of answers, and no-one will be entirely sure their opinion is right. The economic backdrop thus provides a range within which the currency can move. The exact level on any particular day will be influenced by other factors, such as the movement of short-term speculative flows in response to rumours or government statements. The market is also dynamic; what happened to sterling yesterday may well influence expectations about its performance today.

The tools with which the central banks manage the currency markets can be seen in this light. Government statements reinforcing its commitment to the ERM and central bank intervention can stem short-term speculative pressures against a currency. Indeed, the European Monetary System has well-defined responses to temporary squalls in the currency markets. But when a currency's true value lies decisively outside the ERM grid, then a policy response is required. Recent experience suggests that the EMS institutions are failing to provide a balanced framework within which the appropriate policy responses can be co-ordinated.

Free capital flows and interest rates

The problem of managing the currency markets has been made more difficult by the removal of restrictions on capital flows. A company in Italy is now free to move its money out of a lira deposit account into a Deutschmark account even if it has no intention of doing business with Germany. If the company makes the decision for the year ahead, it will compare:

- the one-year lira interest rate
- the one-year Deutschmark interest rate + the expected appreciation of Deutschmark vs lira over the coming year.

If the latter is greater, it will earn more by converting its lire into Deutschmarks, waiting for a year, and then converting them back when the Deutschmark buys more lire. Italian interest rates must exceed those in Germany to an extent which covers the market's estimate of likely lira weakness. If they do not, funds will flow out of the lira until the interest rate is sufficiently large. Within the ERM, interest rate differentials are rather like a thermometer indicating the degree to which the market has confidence in the grid. If the width of the ERM band is $4\frac{1}{2}$ per cent, but the one-year interest rate differential is 10 per cent, then there is clearly an important risk of a realignment. The next section reviews the narrowing of these differentials through the 1980s.

In the early 1980s, controls over investment flows were common across Europe. A borrower of Italian lire in Italy would pay a lower rate from that paid by a currency trader borrowing lire in London. As traders selling lire for speculative reasons must borrow at this higher rate, it would be pushed up by the authorities to help defend the currency. In early 1986, 3-month lira rates in London touched 20 per cent while those in Milan were still at 15 per cent. As part of their commitment to open markets, EC finance ministers have sanctioned the removal of capital controls, with the exception of Greece which is scheduled to lift them at end-1995. Interest rate increases now have an immediate and direct impact on the domestic borrowers and cannot be sustained at penal levels. This aspect of EC policy toward the financial markets has strengthened the hand of the speculators.

What happens when realignments are necessary

Before Maastricht put a new gloss on the Exchange Rate Mechanism, there was no intention that it should be a regime of fixed exchange rates. Indeed, the first realignment occurred just six months after the EMS's inception. Realignments do not in themselves represent a failure of this system, although to preserve its credibility they should clearly not happen too often. The new parities are agreed by all the EC finance ministers and set with the advice of the EC Monetary Committee which includes both finance ministry and central bank officials. As with many aspects of the EMS's operation, whilst the formal procedures are largely fixed, the precise chain of events can differ markedly according to circumstances. The first realignment occurred at the initiative of Germany; the departure of sterling from the ERM grid presented as a fait accompli.

PRE-MAASTRICHT: A DECADE OF RELATIVE STABILITY

The 1979 reforms heralded a new era in European management of the currency markets. The central section of this book deals with the broader economic implications of pegging exchange rates but on the assumption that this is desirable, the European Monetary System had been a great success. Figure 1.2 illustrates the pattern of realignments from March 1979 until the Maastricht agreement in later 1991. The height of the bars indicate the extent of the depreciation of the weakest currency against the strongest, while their spacing reflects the time between each realignment.

The first four years of the System, brought seven realignments with their magnitude marginally greater in 1983 than in 1979. The commitment to stable exchange rates failed to effectively constrain national policy-makers over this period. The 1983 realignment proved a turning point for the System, as it was accompanied by more prudent economic policies in France and institutional change in Italy. Realignments became infrequent and Italy was able to narrow its fluctuation band from $+/- 6$ per cent to $+/- 2\frac{1}{4}$ per cent.

Exchange rate stability was now in the mainstream of the trend towards greater EC integration. While the 1970s approach to currency management had gradually lost members over time, the European Monetary System added them. New currencies were included in the EMS as the Community expanded southward, the Spanish peseta entered the ERM grid in 1989, followed by sterling in 1990 and the escudo in 1992. The

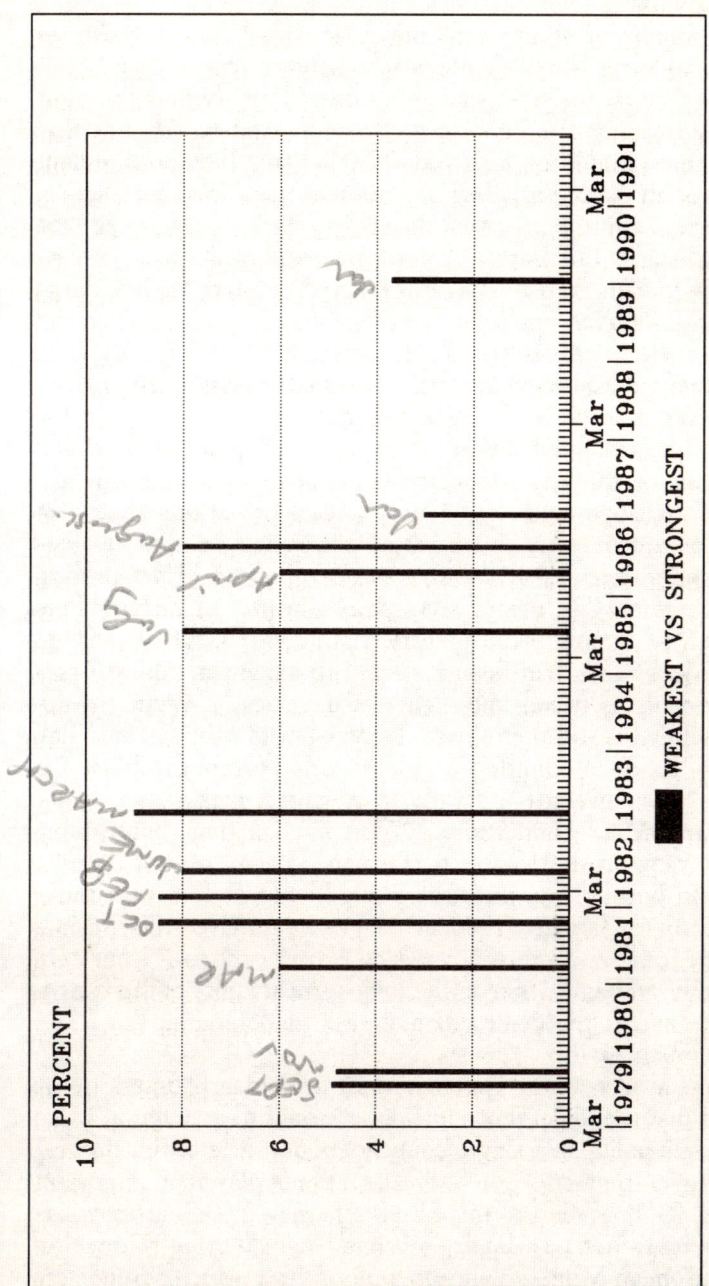

Figure 1.2 ERM realignments before Maastricht

success of the EMS was further endorsed by countries outside the EC linking their currencies to the ECU.

An important strength of the EMS has been its ability to evolve to meet the difficulties which have arisen in practice. Any regime of pegged exchange rates not only requires a set of rules governing the behaviour of the central banks, but that these rules should be followed. The January 1987 realignment occurred in particularly heated circumstances amid accusations that the Bundesbank was doing too little to dampen the Deutschmark. The Basle–Nyborg agreement of that year opened the way for central banks to draw on credit lines to finance intra-marginal intervention (that is before a cross rate reaches the edge of the band). It also gave a greater role for the ECU in repayment of short-term credits. Until the Maastricht agreement, the procedure for realignments had worked reasonably well with sustained intervention as a prelude to weekend meetings of the EC Monetary Committee to decide on new parities. Realignments had been followed by periods of relative stability and, indeed, the weakest currencies prior to realignment were temporarily the strongest in the new grid following it. (A summary of the pre-Maastricht history of realignments is given in Appendix 2.) Investor confidence in the Exchange Rate Mechanism had been reflected in narrowing interest rate differentials between the strong currencies, particularly the Deutschmark, and the other currencies within the system. The best indicator of confidence in long-term currency stability lies in the gap between bond yields. Investors choosing between a 10-year DMark bond and a 10-year French franc bond, must take a view on the franc's performance over the next decade. German bond yields in January 1992 were in line with those prevailing in January 1980 at $8\frac{1}{8}$ per cent. Over this period, French franc and lira yields fell by $3\frac{1}{2}$ per cent and 3 per cent respectively. Confidence in the long-term stability of the system in turn makes the central banks' task of defending the ERM limits much easier.

Some aspects of the system haven't worked as planned. It was hoped that the 'divergence indicator' would trigger action when economic policy in a single country got out of line with the rest of Europe. In practice, the indicator has not played an important role in the operation of the ERM. The new ECU currency has also been rather side-lined — it has a bookkeeping role within the European Monetary Co-operation Fund (which administers

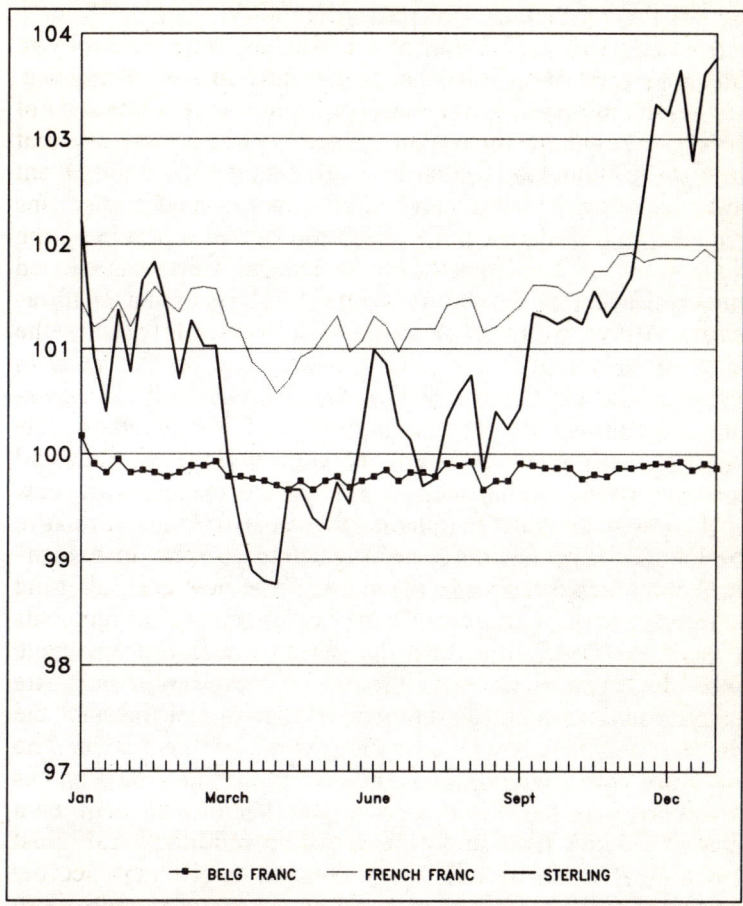

Figure 1.3 Deutschmark's external value in 1991 ERM central rate = 100

the short-term credit lines) but has been little used for direct intervention.

The ERM had been a symmetrical framework — without a single anchor currency — by design. However, in practice, the Deutschmark quickly assumed the role of key currency within the system. When a currency came under downward pressure it was particularly important if its cross rate against the Deutschmark was pressing against the ERM limit. Eventually currencies such as the Belgian franc were kept within even narrower bands around the DMark central rate than the rules of the System demanded. Figure 1.3 illustrates how the operation of the Exchange Rate Mechanism brought widely different degrees of exchange rate stability for European currencies. Throughout 1991, the Belgian franc traded within a ½ per cent of its central rate against the Deutschmark — this along with the Dutch guilder were considered 'core' currencies. Over this period, the French franc traded within its narrow 2¼ per cent band — it along with the Irish punt and the Danish krone were in an intermediate bloc. Finally, sterling/DMark remained relatively volatile within the ERM and was included in the lowest grade of ERM currencies.

The role of the Deutschmark in the ERM was both a strength and a weakness. It can be regarded as a strength as the Bundesbank is providing a non-inflationary anchor to the ERM currencies, which other systems of pegged exchange rates (such as the post-war dollar standard) have lacked. A devaluation of the Deutschmark has never been required. On the other hand, the hoped for symmetry in the system, with both central banks countering pressure on a particular exchange rate, has not come to fruition. The central bank defending a weak currency still bears the greater part of the burden, and substantial increases in interest rates may be required. An analysis of international interest rates makes this asymmetry very clear. When realignment pressures have developed, the interest rates paid on the weak currencies have risen very sharply while Deutschmark rates have edged only fractionally lower. As a result, it can be argued that the ERM has become very similar to its predecessors, but with the Deutschmark, rather than gold or the dollar, at its heart. If realignments are to be ultimately phased out and Germany is setting interest rates to meet its domestic requirements, the monetary policy in the Community may be excessively deflationary.

HOW THE AUTHORITIES 'POLICE' THE GRID

Responses to currency pressures

Following the failure of efforts to stabilise European currencies in the 1970s, the European Monetary System was designed to reinforce the authorities' influence over the currency markets. Central banks and governments throughout the world adopt a range of tools to manage developments in their exchange rate. These often occur in increasing order of seriousness as the downward pressure on a currency intensifies as follows:

- *Talk tough*: the authorities stress the importance of currency, threaten action to defend the exchange rate and attach personal credibility to the policy.
- *'Massage' the markets*: very short-term interest rates may be nudged higher and small-scale intervention undertaken to dampen speculation. These are discrete signals to dealers of official disquiet.
- *Borrow in foreign currencies*: these funds may be used to finance intervention or general public spending, but in either case they will be more expensive to repay in domestic currency terms if there is a devaluation (Sterling repayment = Loan in DMarks divided by sterling/DMark rate).
- *Intervene heavily*: if a central bank is committed to defending a particular level, it has to stand ready to buy all of its currency which the market wishes to sell at that exchange rate. In this operation it is running down its holdings of foreign currencies, and if the support is unsuccessful these must ultimately be replenished at a more expensive rate. Heavy intervention will also have dramatic implications for domestic money supply.
- *Increase interest rates*: the authorities may be forced, finally, to push up interest rates sharply. This action has a dual impact:
  - it improves the rate of return on the currency thus making it more attractive for investors and more expensive for market speculators to sell.
  - it signals a tighter economic policy which may eventually help the country's trade position and thus its currency.

Central banks often adopt special tactics to allow an extremely sharp rise in interest rates for the currency markets, without a corresponding rise in domestic rates. Thus the Irish central bank was able to push up very short-term rates to 100 per cent in late 1992 to defend the punt.

- *Capital controls*: often primarily aimed at market speculators, the central bank regulates the currency activities of banks, companies and even individuals to slow sales of the currency.

However, EC competition rules mean that this step should be taken only as a last resort.

■ *Alter economic policy/institutional changes*: currency crises are often initially treated as a temporary market measure, driven by market speculators. However, the government concerned may finally have to accept there is a fundamental contradiction between currency stability and its other economic targets. Later in this book, we examine profound changes in the process of Italian wage-bargaining required to stabilise the lira in the mid-1980s.

How the EMS helps

It is clearly vital that if the ERM is to be effective, the obligation of central banks to intervene at the limits must be backed up by sufficient fire-power. The EMS included a Very Short Term Financing Facility (VSTF) to deal with this problem. When a cross rate hits a bilateral limit, there is automatic credit from the other central banks to finance intervention *without limit*. In theory, no central bank ever runs out of reserves in the short term. Borrowing under this arrangement should be repaid within three months, although a certain amount can be carried forward for up to a further six months. In recent years, this facility has also been used to finance intervention close to the edge of the ERM bands, but there is no formal obligation to provide credit for this 'intra-marginal' intervention.

It is important to recognise that the unlimited borrowing facility doesn't solve the problem of exchange rate management. This is because of the link between intervention and money supply. The latter is simply a measure of the amount of currency in the hands of the private sector. If the central banks are buying lira from banks, then its supply is contracting; when they sell Deutschmarks, the Bundesbank is faced with a more rapid monetary expansion. Indeed, in one week in September 1992 intervention-related inflows into Germany reached DM 24bn, leaving the Bundesbank according to its President 'no longer in a position to continue our monetary policy'. The central bank could try and offset this expansionary shock through selling government bonds which have to be paid for in domestic currency — this is known in the jargon as 'sterilizing intervention'. The net effect of this is that the Bundesbank has borrowed

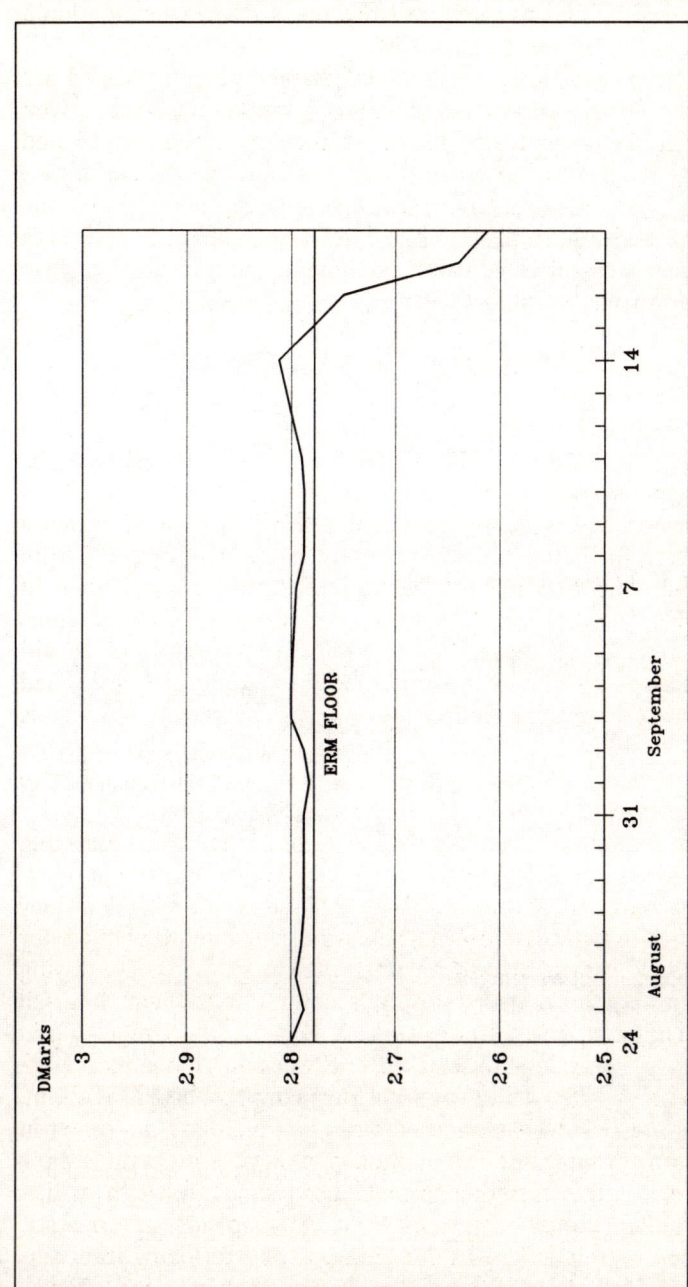

Figure 1.4 Sterling/Deutschmark in Autumn 1992

Table 1.3   The final weeks of Sterling's ERM membership

	United Kingdom	Germany
24	John Major returns from holiday	
25		
26	Lamont statement outside Treasury to remove any 'scintilla of doubt' that sterling to be devalued Intervention totals £1 billion	
27		
28		
29		
30		
31		
1 September		
2		
3	UK Treasury borrows 10 billion ECUs	
4		
5	Bath Meeting: EC Finance Ministers Rule Out EC Realignment	Bundesbank agrees not to raise rates
6		Buba President says he cannot make his true feelings on desirability of realignment public
7		
8		
9		
10	Prime Minister reiterates devaluation would be a 'betrayal'	
11	UK inflation falls to 3.6 per cent	
12		
13	Lira devaluation of 7 per cent announced	
14		Bundesbank cuts money market rates $\frac{1}{2}$ per cent: first rate cut for five years.
15		
16	Heavy intervention at the ERM limit	

United Kingdom	*Germany*
17 Minimum Lending Rate re-introduced 2 per cent increase in rates, further 3 per cent announced £10 bln spent on intervention Suspends membership of ERM	

money in its own debt markets, and then lent it to the Banque de France, or whoever, with the foreign central bank accepting the currency risk. Sterilized intervention doesn't involve any major re-think in monetary policy for either central bank and thus by itself tends to be ineffective. All the central banks within the EMS may draw on two additional sources of financial help. The Short-Term Monetary Support arrangement gives assistance (lasting for nine months) in the case of temporary balance of payments difficulties. The Medium-Term Financial Support facility has proved to be more important in providing longer term help — it provides conditional loans for between two and five years.

The rules of the Exchange Rate Mechanism stress the joint responsibility to ensure the target ranges are observed. In theory, if the Spanish peseta/sterling cross is at the limit then there is an onus on both the Bank of Spain and the Bank of England to act. It was hoped that this burden-sharing would help ensure the stability of the system. The ERM grid also carries with it the full authority of the EC Finance ministers and central banks, and this ideally should reinforce the credibility of the central banks caught up in any temporary squall. Devaluation within the system is a very public admission of the authorities' defeat, and thus it increases the political cost of a U-turn.

When the European finance ministers met in Bath, England on 5 September 1992 they agreed on a statement that the earlier decision 'not to proceed to a realignment in the European Monetary System has been confirmed'. Within two weeks, sterling had temporarily suspended its membership of the

Exchange Rate Mechanism following irresistible pressure on the Sterling/DMark cross rate (see Figure 1.4). From the detailed chronology of Table 1.3 one can see all the measures for managing the currency markets outlined above and judge the 'symmetry' of the EMS in operation. To understand fully the background to this failure, however, we must first turn to the Maastricht Treaty and what it had to say on the controversial question of monetary union.

WHAT WAS AGREED AT MAASTRICHT?

●●

MAASTRICHT AND EUROPEAN INTEGRATION

Following the signing of the Maastricht Treaty in February 1992, political leaders across Europe expressed their support for its terms. The political establishment in Denmark, Ireland and France enthusiastically endorsed a 'yes' vote in their national Maastricht referenda. This rather disguises the fact that the Treaty was the culmination of an intense debate about the nature of the new, integrated Europe. There was no doubt that EC countries were willing to make a major step forward in creating closer European ties, but on what terms? The inter-governmental conferences charged with formulating the new Treaty received widely differing proposals from EC governments. There were two related issues which had to be clarified: the f-word, federalism; and subsidiarity (see box).

There was a marked contrast between the degree of progress in the area of Economic and Monetary Union (EMU) and that of European Political Union (EPU). There had been an important step forward in planning for EMU with the decision to set up the Delors Committee in mid-1988. Its Report advocated a 'quantum jump' in economic and monetary union which, it argued, would secure a significant increase in economic welfare in the community. The process toward a single currency was broken down into a series of steps, and this formed the basis for the Maastricht Treaty's approach to EMU. The path to EMU was a battlefield for the federalists and their opponents. The United Kingdom advocated the creation of a new 'hard'

Federalism and subsidiarity

Federalism   The role which the supra-national institutions would play in determining policy for the European Union. Would the directly elected European Parliament take decisions on pan-European defence policy, or would this be left to the European Council made up of government representatives? Germany and the Netherlands favoured an increase in the power of federal EC institutions, but this was opposed by France and the UK. In the end, any explicit mention of 'federalism' was removed from the Treaty. There is an enhanced role for the European Commission and Parliament, but the inter-governmental Council has powers of review in some areas (such as regional policy) and dominance in others (such as defence).

Subsidiarity   What areas of national life should the European Commission be legitimately trying to influence? The concept of subsidiarity was developed to tackle this problem and enshrined in the Treaty. The Community shall take action 'only if and in so far as the objective of the proposed action cannot be sufficiently achieved by the Member States ... and be better achieved by the Community'. This put the onus on the EC institutions to justify their intervention in national affairs, and further hindered the creation of a single federal European State.

ECU, alongside national currencies, which would hold its value and companies could have the freedom to use (or disregard) as they wished. In this area of policy, the federalists won the day and the planned institutional framework for European monetary union is outlined in this chapter. By the time the Maastricht summit was held in December 1991, the first steps along the Delors path to a single currency had already been taken.

In contrast, progress toward political union had been hesitant. The role of the EC was extended into new areas, such as defence policy, and the 'Citizenship of the European Union' created. But the wholesale institutional reforms necessary to create a powerful European Parliament had not been undertaken. In retrospect, the imbalance between the detailed timetable for EMU and the lack of progress in political union may appear disturbing. For the moment, Europe was set on concentrating on existing strengths — building on the achievements of the European Economic Community and the European Monetary System.

ECONOMIC POLICY IN THE TREATY

One area of the Maastricht negotiations which attracted little controversy was setting out the objectives for economic policy within the EC. The shopping list of aims which economic and monetary union were to promote included:

- A harmonious and balanced development of economic activities.
- Sustainable and non-inflationary growth respecting the environment.
- A high degree of convergence of economic performance.
- A high level of employment and social protection.
- The raising of the standard of living and quality of life.
- Economic and social cohesion and solidarity among Member States.

It is noteworthy that bringing the performance of EC economies into line was regarded as desirable in its own right, not just as a pre-condition for creating a single currency. The Maastricht Treaty also very much retains the free market thrust of the European Economic Community. Member governments are to act in accordance with the principle of 'an open market economy with free competition'.

Is a new pan-European economic policy needed? Given the high degree of economic inter-dependence within the Community, pan-European co-operation is clearly desirable. The Treaty makes provision for 'broad guidelines' for economic policy to be drawn up at the pan-European level. Individual member states will refer to these when setting their policy. The European Commission is given the job of recommending what these guidelines should be, and the European Parliament is informed of what they are. But ultimately the buck stops with the Heads of State meeting in the European Council.

The Treaty's approach to budgetary policy in individual countries fits neatly into this guideline approach. Initially warnings from the centre indicate that budgetary policy may be a little too reckless. Ultimately sanctions may have to be imposed. In contrast, there will be a profound transformation in the conduct of European monetary policy. The Delors plan for monetary union envisaged a three-stage timetable which would end with a single currency and a powerful pan-European institution — the European Central Bank. The new single currency is yet to be formally named. This book follows the Maastricht Treaty and assumes the single currency will be known as 'the ECU'. The Maastricht Treaty thus adopts the following timetable:

Progress toward a single currency

Stage One: Member States remove restrictions on capital flows and make progress in economic convergence

Stage Two: *Begins Jan 1994*
European System of Central Banks (ESCB) created with European Monetary Institute (EMI) at centre. National central banks given independence by governments and co-ordinate within EMI.

Stage Three: *Begins after Jan 1997, by Jan 1999*
The ECU irrevocably fixed against qualifying currencies. European Central Bank runs monetary policy in ECU area. Eventually, the ECU replaces national currencies.

THE TIMETABLE EXPLAINED

The initial steps toward monetary union appear rather innocuous. The EC commitment to free competition in open markets is reflected in Stage One, with a requirement to remove capital controls. This step had been endorsed by a Madrid meeting a year earlier, and Spain and Portugal, the only ERM countries maintaining major controls, were hoping to dispense with them relatively quickly. The removal of capital controls was not controversial but, as Chapter 3 explains, it may well have intensified speculative pressures within the ERM. The Treaty also requires Member States at this stage to adopt long-term economic programmes to create the 'lasting convergence necessary' for monetary union, particularly in the areas of price stability and sound public finances.

The step to Stage Two will occur at a fixed date: 1 January 1994, and establishes a new independent European body. The European Monetary Institute will take over some tasks within the EMS, such as administrating intervention finance, but its primary importance lies in improving policy co-ordination and making detailed plans for Stage Three. During Stage Two, the Member States will also ensure that their central banks each conform to the new pan-European standards in terms of independence.

Delors' 'quantum jump' in monetary union occurs at the beginning of Stage Three. And it is on the nature of this jump that the major decisions were taken at Maastricht. At this point, the European Central Bank (ECB) will replace the EMI, and manage monetary policy for the single currency area. The ECB and the national central banks will be linked together in the European System for Central Banks and will follow ECB instructions. This is rather like the US Federal Reserve System with the regional banks simply implementing the policy decisions of the central Federal Reserve Board. The parities between the ECU and the qualifying national currencies (and thus the bilateral exchange rates) will become irrevocably fixed. The Bundesbank, the Banque de France et al will give up their authority to set monetary conditions to the ECB.

At present there are wide differences in the role of central banks across Europe. The degree of autonomy ranges from the high degree of independence of the Bundesbank to the subservience to politicians of the Bank of England. The Bundesbank has an explicit obligation to seek price stability, while the Bank of England's management of monetary policy will change at each election. It is not too surprising that the Bundesbank wished to ensure that the European Central Bank would be as committed to fighting inflation as the Bundesbank itself has been. Indeed, the negotiations ahead of Maastricht revealed a consensus that the new monetary union should be one of low inflation and conservative budgetary policies. Details on three key issues were settled in the Treaty:

- Who would run the new ECB, and what would be its responsibilities?
- Which countries would be involved in monetary union at its inception?
- When would the ECB take the reins of European monetary policy?

The European Central Bank (and the ECSB)

In a Treaty where the language tends to be long-winded and heavy with sub-clauses, the section on monetary policy begins with a blunt statement: 'The primary objective of the ECSB shall be to maintain price stability'.

It then allows the central bank to try to achieve other economic objectives (outlined in the last section) as long as price stability is not prejudiced. This follows the model of the Bundesbank's legislative requirement to seek price stability.

The Bundesbank model is also followed in granting the new central bank independence. The Treaty specifies that '. . . neither the ECB, nor a national central bank, nor any member of their decision-making bodies shall seek or take instructions from Community institutions or bodies, from any government of a Member State, or any other body'. It also calls on governments to act in good faith and respect this principle, perhaps recognising that the establishment of independent central banks represents a major change for many European countries. Immediate, direct democratic control over the level of interest rates is voluntarily being given up.

The ECB will have all the powers of a traditional central bank — setting interest rates and authorising note issuance. It was decided that it will be run by an Executive Council composed of six members with 'recognized standing and professional experience' in the areas of money and banking. Apart from excluding amateur central bankers — and the fact that everyone is consulted over their appointment — the Treaty has little else to say on this matter. The Board members serve for eight years. The national central bank Governors sit alongside the six Executive members in the Governing Council of the ECB and it is here that the real power lies. The Governing Council formulates monetary policy; taking decisions on money supply targets and key interest rates. The Executive Board is responsible for implementing monetary policy, but within the guidelines set down by the Governing Council.

The ECB reports to the Council and the European Parliament on its activities. As with the US Federal Reserve and the German Bundesbank, the central bank cannot be completely independent. Whatever the precise constitutional position outlined in the Treaty, the ECB will in the end be answerable to European and Member parliaments. The Treaty makes clear, however, that national central bank governors are not to be simply representatives of national government interests. It not only specifies their minimum tenure (five years) but outlines in some detail the circumstances in which they can be fired.

Who joins the single currency area?

If the single currency area was established with high-inflation Greece as a founding member then clearly the ECB's aim of price stability would be a distant goal. Perhaps this goal would eventually be compromised as pressures to reduce the real value of government debts through higher inflation became overwhelming. To ensure that the single currency area starts out with low inflation and prudent budgetary policies, the Maastricht Treaty sets criteria by which new applicants to the area will be judged (see box). Targets for each measure of suitability are outlined, and although they are not absolute minimum standards the wording of the Treaty strongly suggests that they should be met. Ultimately, the Commission and ECB prepare reports and the final decision rests with the Heads of State. The stringency of these standards is to be judged by the fact that even the strong-currency countries such as Belgium and the Netherlands fail to meet all these standards and must undergo a period of adjustment. For Greece they are a distant objective. Setting high standards for the countries embarking on EMU meant that a degree of flexibility had to be built into the Maastricht timetable.

EMU entry standards

CRITERION — Price stability
STANDARD: Over the past year the Member State has inflation which does not exceed by more than 1½ percentage points the average of the three best performing States. The fall in inflation to this level should be sustainable.

CRITERION — Budgetary policy
STANDARD: The Commission should not have judged that the State has an 'excessive deficit' in its budget. Ideally, the government deficit will be running at less than 3 per cent of national output and outstanding government debt will represent less than 60 per cent of output. If the actual figures have fallen substantially and 'come close' to these values, this may be sufficient.

CRITERION — ERM membership
STANDARD: The Membership State should have maintained its currency within a narrow band for at least two years 'without severe tensions' and without initiating a devaluation.

CRITERION — Long-term interest rates
STANDARD: In the year prior to the entry request, average long-term interest rates should not exceed by more than 2 percentage points the average for the three best performing Member States in terms of price stability.

How distant is the single currency objective?

Setting a start date for Stage Two of EMU was relatively straight-forward. The European Monetary Institute will be established in early 1994, and any countries which have yet to remove capital controls will be allowed to continue along the EMU road (they receive a 'derogation'). The beginning of Stage Three is more problematic as no-one is certain when there will be enough countries meeting the required standards. The Treaty states that:

- Until the end of 1997, the Heads of Government can set a start date for Stage Three if they judge that a majority of economies meet the necessary conditions. The final decision is taken by a 'qualified majority' in the European Council — where the votes are weighted to reflect each Government's relative importance.
- Otherwise, Stage Three will start on 1 January 1999 with only those countries that do qualify participating in the single currency area.

After this date there are bi-annual reviews to allow for the remaining countries to be included when they finally come up to scratch. Eventually, at some unspecified date in the next millenium, the ECU (carrying the profile of Jacques Delors) may circulate as the single currency of the 'European Union'.

Our discussion of the ECB's role suggests that while the 'ECU club' may be exclusive, joining involves a major relinquishment of democratic control over interest rates. The right of the United Kingdom not to proceed to Stage Three is explicitly recognised in a Treaty Protocol. Denmark also reserves the right to drop out following a referendum. For many EC economies, however, the Maastricht Treaty represented a major new impetus to economic adjustment and restructuring rather than a threat to national sovereignty.

WHERE EC COUNTRIES STOOD AT END 1991

The setting of a firm start date for Stage Three and demanding entry standards ensured that there would be a tiered approach to monetary union. Indeed, the day of the Maastricht summit saw newspaper headlines such as 'Tiers on the road to an EC currency union.' This fact appears to have been forgotten in recent debates over whether there will be a two-tier or two-speed Europe. Table 2.1 outlines how the EC economies stood relative to the Maastricht targets at the end of 1991. The three best performing countries have an average inflation rate of $2\frac{3}{4}$ per cent, which puts the inflation objective at $4\frac{1}{4}$ per cent. Bond yields in these countries are around 9 per cent, so yields in new entrants to the ECU area should be no higher than 11 per cent. Compared with the Treaty criteria, the economies at this point fell into three broad groupings:

- Denmark, France, Luxembourg and Germany had no or little adjustment to make. Of this group only the German fiscal deficit was of concern, and would have to be kept under a tight rein.
- Greece had to make substantial progress in both budgetary policy and inflation. Despite its long-term membership of the ERM, Italy's budgetary problems demanded major policy changes, while further steps to reduce Portuguese inflation were required.
- In the mid-ground there were a group of countries which could well be among the founding members of the ECU area, but which required sustained prudence in monetary and budgetary policy in the first half of the decade. If the standards on government debt were to be applied strictly then Belgium, Ireland and the Netherlands would have to sharply reduce public spending (or raise taxes) in order to qualify.

An interesting exercise is to compare how the financial markets regarded the currencies at this point, with their standing under their Maastricht criteria. Market confidence in a currency can be judged by short-term interest rate differentials where capital controls have been removed. In the final quarter of 1991, relative to Deutschmark 3-month interest rates, the differentials over German rates were as follows:

Spain	3.34
Italy	2.67
United Kingdom	1.21
France	.53
Denmark	.32
Ireland	.28
Netherlands	.12
Belgium	.10

Portuguese and Greek rates were well above those in Spain. It appears that the debt over-hang in some EC countries, such as Belgium, had not undermined confidence in currency stability. A long-established commitment to ERM membership and closely following German monetary policy changes may explain this. It is noteworthy that while France's prudent policies had reduced inflation and government deficits below German levels,

Table 2.1 EC countries and the Maastricht standards end 1991

Little or no adjustment required

	Target	Denmark	France	Germany	Luxemb
Inflation (%)	4¼	2¼	2¾	4	3
Govt deficit (%)	3	1½	1¾	3	−2
Govt debt (%)	60	60	47	48	6½
ERM membership	24 mnths	met	met	met	met
Long yields (%)	11	8¾	8½	8¼	9

Some adjustment required

	Target	Belgium	Britain	Nethlnds	Ireland	Spain
Inflation (%)	4¼	3	4¼	3¾	3½	6
Govt deficit (%)	3	5½	2	4	4	3¾
Govt debt (%)	60	130	38	80	110	46
ERM membership	24 mnths	met	wide bnd	met	met	wide bnd
Long yields (%)	11	9	9½	8¾	8¾	11¾

Major adjustment required

	Target	Italy	Portugal	Greece
Inflation (%)	4¼	6	10	18
Govt deficit (%)	3	10	4¾	16
Govt debt (%)	60	105	65	85
ERM membership	24 mnths	23 mnths	none	none
Long yields (%)	11	11¼	17	not avail

Govt deficit — as percentage of national output
Govt debt — outstanding debt as percentage of national output
Figures rounded to simplify comparison

French rates still remained 50 basis points above Deutschmark rates.

What did the EMU timetable mean for a country like Italy? As one of the original Group of Six countries which signed the original 1957 Treaties, it represented both a threat and an opportunity. The threat was that Italy would be left behind, relegated to second-tier and no longer be at the heart of Europe. The opportunity was that these targets could provide an external stimulus to domestic change. The fear of being left behind could force a domestic political consensus for dramatic action to tackle urgent economic problems. Given their progress since joining the EC, Spain and Portugal were also intent on meeting, or approaching, the Treaty standards over the next five years. With countries such as Austria, Switzerland and Sweden expressing an interest in joining the EC, there was strong pressure on existing members to position themselves for Stage Three of monetary union. A German official at the summit explained 'We want to avoid at all costs the possibility that (economically) unserious countries could form a blocking minority which would hold up EMU'.

Within two months of the Treaty being signed, Portugal entered the escudo into the Exchange Rate Mechanism. The initial post-summit enthusiasm for European integration was reflected in a planned 'rush to converge' for the EC economies. There are convincing arguments that this approach was flawed, and might have ultimately derailed the European integration train. Fortunately the Danish referendum introduced a degree of pragmatism and meant short-term policy decisions would not be dominated by the 'demands' of European integration.

MAASTRICHT AND THE EXCHANGE RATE MECHANISM

The successful negotiation of the Maastricht Treaty made no immediate changes to the way the European Monetary System operated. However, it had a profound impact on how the ERM was viewed by the financial markets and European central bankers.

Firstly it increased confidence that measures to produce economic convergence would be implemented throughout Europe. This was despite mounting evidence that progress toward economic convergence was stalling. Many national authorities had adopted multi-year plans, but the outcomes were not matching expectations. Spanish inflation is a good example. It was targeted to fall from 8 per cent in 1986 to 3 per cent in 1989. In actual fact, having fallen sharply due to lower oil prices in 1986 it then rebounded to 6 per cent and stuck there. As a result Spanish wage agreements in 1990 were no lower than they had been five years earlier. Italian budget deficits continually overshot official projections, but the markets believed this would be sorted out — the political cost of falling behind in Europe was simply too high.

Secondly from its inception the ERM had been a system of pegged exchange rates, with periodic realignments. But with the rejection of the British 'hard ECU' plan, ERM stability became a vital step on the road to monetary union. The minimum standards for joining the ECU club included a stipulation that the member's currency must have observed the normal fluctuation margins of the System for at least two years, without the member initiating a devaluation. Naturally, there must be some political cost associated with a request to realign the central rates, otherwise the system would not be stable. But following Maastricht, there was a danger that requesting a realignment meant being left behind on the road to a single currency. Not only would a devaluation directly damage hopes of meeting the ERM criteria, but the Euro-enthusiasts argued it could stall the entire convergence programme.

The first of these influences helped maintain the stability of the System. When speculation against the lira developed on the currency markets, those confident in economic convergence across Europe purchased high-yielding lira bonds. As we will see in the next chapter, however, an unwillingness by politicians to countenance realignments would finally put irresistible pressure on the existing parities.

THE RUSH FOR CONVERGENCE

The Euro-enthusiasts argued that the narrowing of inflation and budget deficit differentials should be engineered relatively quickly. Without this, the momentum for European integration might be lost — a failure to make early progress would thus be a backward step. If the ECU were to be circulating throughout the EC countries in the last years of the 20th century this would be a major step forward in creating a European vision. In the words of the Madrid Council, the single currency would be an expression of the EC's 'identity and unity'.

While this all sounds rather grand and virtuous, the plain reality was that at the beginning of 1992 most of Europe was faced with problems of sluggish economic growth and disturbingly high unemployment. At this point perhaps a co-ordinated policy to promote European growth should have been put in place. Instead, the fiscal and inflation standards set for monetary union require conservative policies in some economies, and contractionary policies in others. For economies with large outstanding public debt, such as Belgium, there must be a major reform in the state of public finances if the limits on government debt are to be strictly applied. The OECD estimates that to meet the limit on public debt by 1998, Belgium would have to trim its public spending by 6 per cent each year over this period. Italy, Spain and Greece would have to adopt heavy counter-inflationary measures to qualify. But it is not the problems of individual countries which is the key concern.

There are strong reasons for believing a period of budgetary retrenchment is required in the European countries concerned. Clearly fiscal retrenchment in Italy, for example, is urgently required. But in the rush for convergence, national policy-makers in the wake of Maastricht were set to act *simultaneously* to adopt more restrictive policies. When all these national decisions are aggregated, pan-European economic policy in the next five years looked set to dampen rather than promote economic growth. Given recent developments in Germany, it appeared that restrictive policies in the rest of Europe would coincide with a renewed tightening of German fiscal policy.

Exactly what would be the unemployment cost of such an adjustment phase? Estimating the total cost requires complicated mathematical models as reduced public expenditure in one country will depress economic growth (and thus tax revenues) elsewhere in Europe. While European Commission estimates of the gains from economic and monetary union are freely available, there is comparative secrecy as to these transition costs. Indeed, in the popular press this has been referred to as the 'hidden cost' of European union. The large model of the world economy at the International Monetary Fund indicated that EC growth would be reduced by around 0.6 per cent over the years 1992–1996 as a result of the adjustment process. Growth in 1993 may be 0.75 per cent lower than would otherwise be the case. Against a backdrop of weak world economic growth, this suggested European unemployment, now at $9\frac{1}{2}$ per cent would remain on an upward trend.

The restructuring of public finances and reduction of inflation across Europe will no doubt provide a suitable backdrop for stronger economic growth over the long-term. The policy adjustments are thus rather like an investment with a short-term cost but long-term benefits. The questions raised by this analogy are:

- Should this pan-European investment occur all at once or by instalments?

■ Do we want to invest now, or when prospects for growth are more favourable?

It may well be regarded as fortuitous that the enthusiasm for pan-European monetary union toward the end of this decade has been dampened by recent EMS developments. Just seven months after the ink dried on the Maastricht Treaty, the Exchange Rate Mechanism was plunged into crisis.

SUMMARY: THE MAASTRICHT AGREEMENT

■ The Maastricht Treaty represents a major stride (the timetable for Economic and Monetary Union) and a small step (the minor modification of EC institutions) in European integration.

■ General economic policy will be overseen by EC 'guidelines' but there is a detailed programme for the adoption of a single currency and surrender of national monetary policies.

■ A European Central Bank will be established at the latest by mid-1998, though only countries meeting certain minimum standards will be within the single currency area, formed by January 1999.

■ Based on these standards, European economies fall into three broad categories and as a result a multi-tiered monetary union became inevitable.

■ Maastricht raised hopes of early action across Europe to promote early economic convergence. Fiscal and monetary policy could well have become significantly more contractionary at a time of disappointing growth and contained inflationary pressures.

Chapter
THREE

THE ROOTS OF THE ERM 'CRISIS'

●●

THE FIRST DEFECTIONS — STERLING AND THE LIRA

The signing of the Maastricht Treaty in February 1992 represented a high point in hopes that there would be speedy progress toward monetary union. From that point onward there were a series of shocks which rocked the European currency markets and appeared in danger of destroying the EMS itself. The failure of the Danish referendum to back the Treaty not only raised fears that the Danes would require some special treatment but tapped a groundswell of opinion across Europe against monetary union. A German opinion poll revealed that a decisive majority of people did not wish to lose the stable Deutschmark in favour of the untested ECU. Against such a backdrop and with German money supply growing disturbingly fast, the Bundesbank had little hesitation in raising its discount rate to a record $8\frac{3}{4}$ per cent.

This move dashed hopes of an early easing of German interest rates to support European economic growth. Following the Danish referendum, the currency markets increasingly concentrated on current economic and political developments in other countries rather than hopes for EMU. As can be seen from Figure 3.1, long-term bond yields paid to holders of ECU bonds (a good indicator of investor's confidence in the prospects for convergence) rose from $8\frac{1}{2}$ per cent to 10 per cent in just six months. Short-term interest rates also edged higher across Europe, and rose sharply in Italy as its political

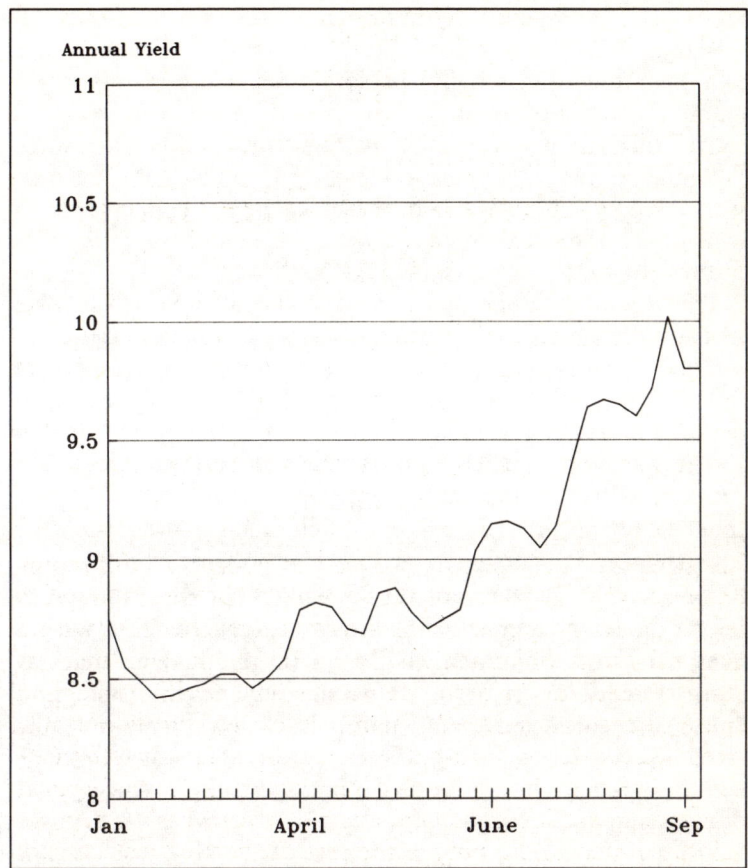

Figure 3.1 ECU bond yield — 1992

crisis deepened. The EC finance ministers' meeting in early September, ruling out a realignment, failed to dampen speculative pressures against the lira which threatened to overwhelm the central banks' willingness to intervene. Finally, in mid-September a deal worked out between Bonn and Rome sanctioned a 7.5 per cent devaluation of the lira and a half point cut in German rates.

This realignment could be viewed as part of the normal operation of the Exchange Rate Mechanism. It was disappointing for the EMU enthusiasts that the realignment had been necessary, but this was balanced by the fact that the Bundesbank had made a rare move to cut rates largely as a result of external pressures. The cut was described by the British Chancellor as 'demonstrating the benefits of continuing close co-operation among Community countries'. But there had not been a smooth ERM realignment — central bank intervention in the prior week had totalled DM 24 bn, a substantial injection into German money supply. This was in a different league to the interventions prior to the 1987 realignment (DM 15bn) and during the 1973 international currency crisis (DM 16bn).

The lira devaluation failed to halt the massive speculative pressure on the currency markets. Within a couple of days, the lira had breached its new floor against the Deutschmark at 820.68 (Figure 3.2). The financial market's lack of confidence in the stability of the system was reflected in the fact that it traded outside the ERM bands during the European day when the central banks intervene at the limits. Sterling also came under heavy downward pressure which failed to ease when the UK Chancellor sanctioned an increase in official rates from 10 per cent to 15 per cent on 15 September. Intervention to defend the pound demanded by the Exchange Rate Mechanism's rules may have amounted to £15 bn (DM 40bn) on that day alone. Finally, at 4pm the Bank of England told its fellow European central bankers that the UK's membership of the ERM was being suspended. Shortly afterwards the Bank of Italy decided to allow the lira to float freely in the currency markets until speculative pressures subsided.

The EC's Monetary Committee met to discuss these events that evening. It noted the UK and Italian decisions, but they had been presented as faits accomplis. Although Britain's appeals to suspend the whole grid were not accepted, some of the basic rules of the ERM appeared to have been swept aside by the pace of events and confidence in the system was severely shaken. A subsequent speculative attack on the French franc was successfully resisted, but disturbingly Spain and Ireland re-introduced capital controls to protect their currencies. Progress in removing capital controls in Stage One of the path to monetary union was in danger of being reversed by the ERM's operational difficulties. Whilst EC rules allowed for the temporary re-introduction of capital controls, they were quickly becoming essential for the system's smooth operation.

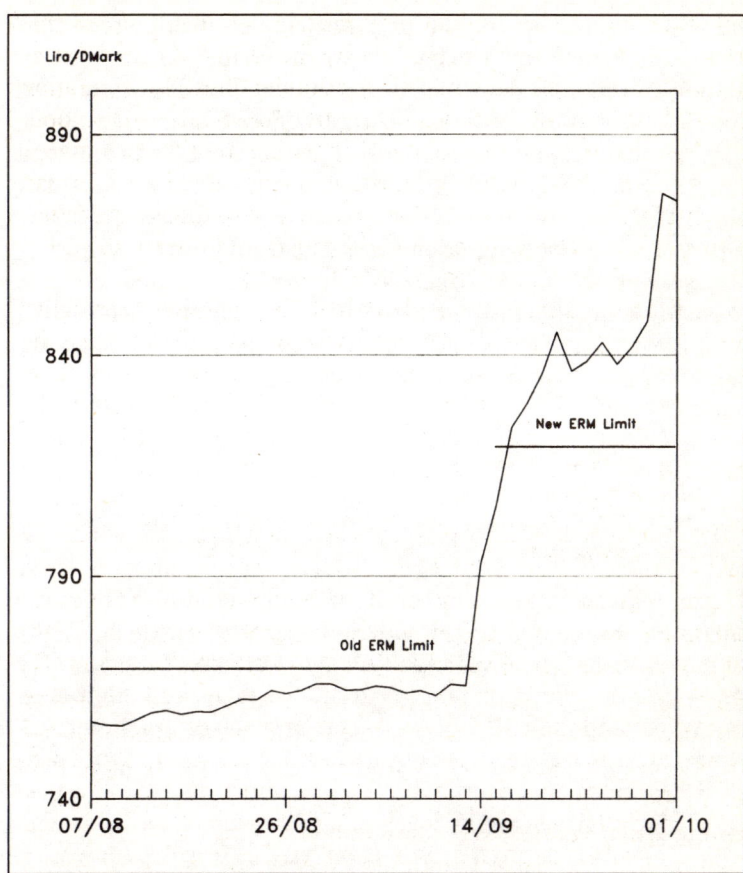

Figure 3.2 Lira/DMark failed realignment

THE ERM AND THE ECONOMIC OUTLOOK

This failure of the EMS was an operational one. A period of stability, improved confidence and expansion had come to a sudden end. But a case can be made that the EMS was not only failing to manage currency fluctuations but also failing in a much broader, and more important, sense. The European Monetary System is a method of international co-operation, where policy actions are often heavily influenced by the rules of the System. As was evident in mid-1992, interest rates may become highly volatile as a result of anchoring currencies and these swings will in turn impact on people's living standards. The Exchange Rate Mechanism must be judged on broader economic grounds than just currency stability. Has it created the right policy incentives and international co-ordination to ensure sustained low-inflation growth within the ERM countries? Throughout 1991 and 1992 there were growing fears that the ERM framework was unnecessarily depressing economic expansion and boosting unemployment throughout Europe.

Assessing the ERM's record is rather complicated as there are many economic indicators to which one can turn. Figure 3.3 summarises the European Community experience through the 1980s for four important indicators:

1. inflation;
2. real GDP growth;
3. unemployment;
4. real short-term interest rates (short-term interest rates less actual inflation).

These indicators are compared with the United States and Japan. Although European inflation appears rather high, the countries within the Exchange Rate Mechanism throughout the 1980s had a better inflation performance than the Community as a whole and the ERM brought convergence of inflation rates. However, this has been at the expense of a rather disappointing growth performance in the 1980s. The most disturbing aspect of this period has been the level of unemployment, which is high both by world standards and from an historical perspective. Given that the ERM is supposed to bear down on inflationary tendencies with a low cost in terms of unemployment, high European unemployment has been surprisingly persistent.

Growth over recent years has been disappointing not only in Europe, but throughout the OECD area. Within Europe, wide divergences in the pace of economic expansion have developed as a result of German reunification. Growth in Germany in 1991 was a healthy 3.2 per cent, but this contrasts with a 1.9 per cent fall in national output in the United Kingdom. Overall Community growth remains relatively sluggish and unemployment may be set to nudge back above 10 per cent for the first time since 1987.

The optimists argue that European co-operation will provide a better response to these policy problems. In fact, the

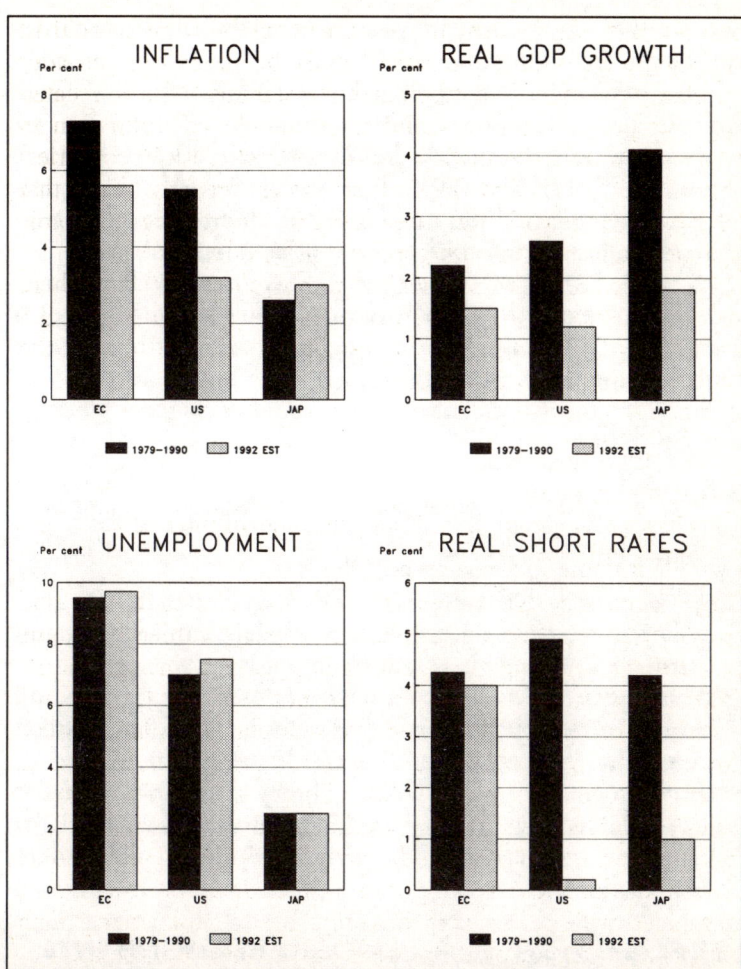

Figure 3.3 Economic performance of the EC compared to US and Japan during the 1980s

ERM-based form of co-ordination appears to have left the German Bundesbank setting interest rates largely on domestic criteria and other European central banks unable to cut their official rates. As the 1992 data in Figure 3.3 indicates, the United States and Japan have responded to weaker growth by substantially cutting real interest rates — in the US they are close to zero. In contrast, European real interest rates remain high as the unemployment picture, already unfavourable by world standards, deteriorates further.

In the week prior to the Italian lira devaluation, the UK Prime Minister gave an important speech, resisting calls for a sterling devaluation. He dismissed the inevitable 'chorus of quack doctors' calling for a reversal of his policy. When pegged currency systems run into problems, it is often political leaders who are the last to recognise that a fundamental problem — not just a market crisis of confidence — has arisen. On our brief review of the evidence, the ERM appears to have undergone an operational failure against a backdrop of disturbing economic trends in the ERM economies. We will now consider four explanations for its current difficulties and consider the necessary action in each case.

- *Explanation 1*: Divergent political and economic changes in Europe, particularly in Germany, demanded currency realignments for sterling and the lira.
- *Explanation 2*: The rules of the ERM aren't creating the best policy outcome for Europe as a whole. A more profound *institutional* change is required urgently.
- *Explanation 3*: Market speculation is increasingly powerful and must be matched by an overhaul in EMS intervention rules. Perhaps capital controls will be necessary.
- *Explanation 4*: The ERM is simply revealing domestic economic failings (such as problems in the labour markets) which need correcting. The macro-economic policy failure is illusory.

EXPLANATION 1 — PERIODIC REALIGNMENTS ARE NECESSARY AND ONE WAS DUE IN 1992

Short-term interest rates adjusted for inflation have remained high in many of the ERM economies despite relatively weak economic growth. Why was the Exchange Rate Mechanism keeping European monetary policy too tight in mid-1992? The answer lies with the role of currency fluctuations, to be outlined in Chapter 4. If an improvement in a country's competitiveness is required due to economic or political shocks then with freely floating exchange rates the currency will adjust downward to a more appropriate level. Within the ERM, there is a more

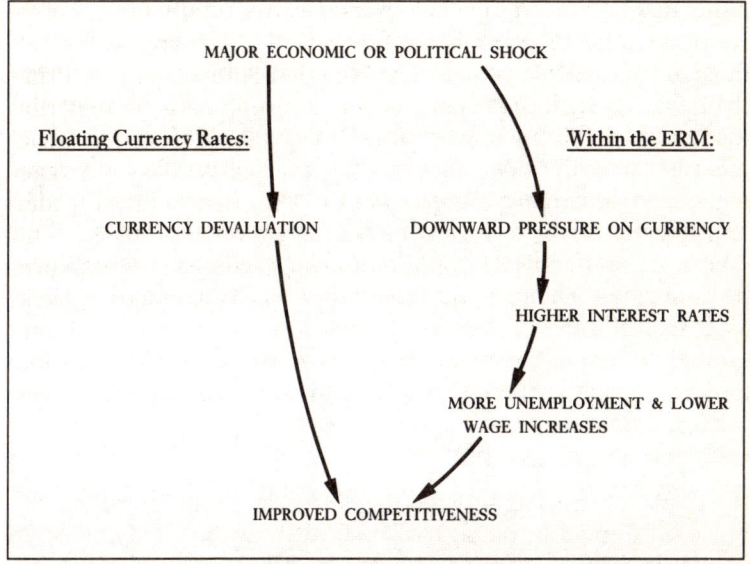

Figure 3.4 The process of achieving improved competitiveness with floating exchange rates and within the ERM

circuitous route to improved competitiveness which is shown in Figure 3.4.

If this analysis is correct then we should be able to trace the source of the economic and political shock. It may be relatively short-lived — these interest rate pressures could simply be encouraging a narrowing of European inflation rates, or may reflect a policy shift which will ultimately be reversed. However, we may also find that currencies have been fundamentally linked up at the wrong level and only a sustained period, perhaps a decade, of high unemployment and real wage cuts will be required before these tensions are resolved. In this case a realignment was indeed the best option, as there was a risk that the ERM (rather like the inter-War Gold Standard) would trigger a sustained slump in some European economies.

A fundamental currency mis-alignment?

Trying to measure whether currencies within the ERM are fundamentally over or under-valued is exceptionally tricky.

Estimates focus on the relative costs of production in two countries, and then predict what level of exchange rates bring these into line. If a country's currency is substantially stronger than this level, its exporters will lose ground in international markets and the trade position will deteriorate. Complications arise because the countries concerned may produce different types of good making comparisons difficult. Alternatively, quality improvements may be offsetting rises in production costs. Often a lack of competitiveness at a particular exchange rate can only be confirmed when the trade deterioration is apparent.

Taking all the evidence into account, on pure competitiveness grounds it cannot be argued that the Deutschmark was uniformly too strong or too weak within the ERM in mid-1992. Instead other currencies could be placed in broad groups according to their relative competitiveness:

- Exporters in Belgium and the Netherlands appeared to have a substantial advantage relative to those in Germany, suggesting their currencies were significantly under-valued. This is reflected by the Netherlands trade surplus which is a healthy 2 per cent of national output.
- The Spanish peseta, Portuguese escudo and Irish punt were also a little 'too weak'. However, issues of product quality and specialisation makes the competitiveness arguments for this group of countries less compelling.
- The French franc was fairly valued, whilst the Danish krone may be viewed as having been fractionally 'too strong'.
- The Italian lira's rating is particularly controversial. On some estimates it was fairly valued but it was running a trade deficit and its share of international markets was edging lower, suggesting over-valuation within the ERM.
- Sterling at its central ERM rate was 10 per cent over-valued, making UK producers uncompetitive in export markets and vulnerable to competition from imports. Reflecting this, the UK current account deficit is running at 2 per cent of GDP despite a substantial down-turn in domestic spending over recent years.

The clearest case, then, was the United Kingdom. If domestic spending recovered without a realignment of sterling, the UK trade deficit looked set to become unsustainably large. Given this, real interest rates had to remain sufficiently high to prevent any recovery occurring. After a long period of economic depression, wages could well have fallen to a level which would make the UK competitive again — at this point growth could resume. Naturally trade flows don't always dominate the currency markets — investment flows are also important. There are long-term factors at work there too and attempts have been made to estimate what currency rates would bring total demand and supply into balance over the long term. These 'Fundamental Equilibrium Real Exchange Rates (FEER)' have been estimated for sterling, and suggest that its over-valuation at DM 2.95 was even larger than earlier estimated.

Conclusion
There is strong evidence to support the view of the Bundesbank that a sterling devaluation, and perhaps a lira devaluation, *were* required on competitiveness grounds. The Bundesbank President's statement that he could not make public his view on the desirability of a realignment simply shook the EMS tree. The ripe fruit fell from its branches.

Was a German policy shock to blame?

For the majority of currencies there does not appear to be a major problem of long-term misalignment. High real official rates in France cannot be traced to a desperate attempt to support an over-valued franc. A second question remains however: is a temporary economic shock causing the problem? There is some evidence pointing in that direction as the dominant ERM economy has undergone a major policy lurch since re-unification.

The process of re-unification was exceptionally rapid. The Berlin wall was opened on 9 November 1989 and by 1 July 1990 the Deutschmark was the sole legal tender in both Germanies. The public funds required to help restructure the eastern länder have proved immense — the annual cost will reach some 6 per cent of national output. Much of this has been financed by borrowing and there has been a major budgetary boost to the west German economy. This, combined with new demand from consumers in the east, has created heavy demand for west German products. Inflationary pressures were inevitable, and with wage settlements running around $6\frac{1}{2}$ per cent in 1991 the Bundesbank progressively tightened monetary policy. The Lombard rate rose from 8 per cent early in 1990 to a peak of $9\frac{3}{4}$ per cent in late 1991.

If the ERM had not existed how would the currency markets have reacted? Over a period of months rather than in the very long-term, the currency acts rather like a 'safety valve' for domestic economic pressures. In contrast to the picture in Germany, demand growth elsewhere in Europe was proving rather sluggish. The Deutschmark may well have appreciated sharply, temporarily exceeding its true long-term value. This rise would have made imports into Germany significantly cheaper, thus cooling inflationary pressure. More of the domestic economic stimulus would have spilled over into the rest of Europe, helping French and Italian growth. This type of currency response was evident in the United States in the early 1980s, when a major fiscal boost and anti-inflationary policies led to a sustained appreciation of the dollar.

With the ERM as a policy strait-jacket, official rates rose throughout Europe as the Bundesbank tightened. Real short-term interest rates — not the German currency — were forced up temporarily in response to the shock and created excess capacity elsewhere in Europe. This is not necessarily a long-term problem for the ERM. At some point the expansion in German public borrowing is likely to be reversed and, as growth slows, Bundesbank interest rates will continue on a downward path. A different currency system could be constructed, with wider 10 per cent bands and scope for regular adjustments. But with the ERM as it is, there is a short-term price to be paid for currency stability — national monetary policy may at times seem entirely inappropriate on domestic grounds. Perhaps the next shock will push French franc rates down to an artificially low level. . . .

Conclusion

High real interest rates outside Germany can be traced to divergent economic policy choices in Europe and the working of the ERM. The Exchange Rate Mechanism didn't cause this divergence and members have a choice of paying this short-term price for currency stability or realigning.

EXPLANATION 2 — PROBLEMS LIE IN THE ERM RULES FOR CO-ORDINATION

Who sets monetary policy for Europe? With a pegged exchange rate system and regular changes in the central rates no-one does. Each country makes its own choices on inflation and the changes in competitiveness due to different inflation rates are offset by realignments. This is how the EMS operated in the early 1980s. Some convergence in economic performance was required, otherwise the frequency of realignments would have undermined the stability of the system. National central banks retained flexibility within limits to set domestic interest rates. However, along the road to monetary union, the EMS evolves into something new. Realignments become increasingly infrequent and a devaluation could threaten a country's chances of joining the single currency area. So who determines European monetary policy now?

With the strongest currencies within the EMS forming the basis of the new ECU club the answer must lie with their central banks, and in particular the Bundesbank. Without realignments, there is a clear transfer of monetary independence to Frankfurt. As a result, the Netherlands has its interest rates largely determined by Germany but has no role in formulating policy. This 'disenfranchisement' is made particularly stark when set against the fact that individual German states have direct representation on the Bundesbank ruling council. It is this problem which was at the heart of the British decision to suspend sterling from the ERM rather than devalue. British officials argued that its commitment to maintain the sterling parity could only be sustained in the context of broader economic policy co-operation across Europe.

But the current situation certainly represents an unsatisfactory 'half-way house' as far as the Bundesbank is concerned. The Bundesbank's goal (enshrined in legislation) is to maintain domestic price stability and only indirectly takes international considerations into account. With inflationary pressures mounting in Germany, the Bundesbank's role has become acutely difficult. On the one hand, other European central banks are unwilling to allow the Deutschmark to be realigned upward thus dampening domestic inflation. This makes a more pronounced rise in German rates inevitable. On the other hand, it comes under international pressure not to raise rates because of the weakness of growth elsewhere. Paradoxically, European policymakers wish to share the reputation of the Bundesbank as an inflation fighter while at the same time diluting that commitment. In the wake of the huge lira-related intervention flows, Helmut Schlesinger, the Bundesbank President, accepted that the German central bank never had 'full independence' in a system of fixed exchange rates.

Within EC budgetary guidelines, the recent German fiscal expansion could well have been less ambitious. With a European Central Bank, interest rates may have been lower across Europe in recent years. Perhaps a large EC budget would have redistributed resources to the weaker EC economies. Would a more uniform pattern of economic expansion across Europe with lower average unemployment have been the result? This is now a matter for speculation. Recent experience suggests, however, that a *durable* fixed exchange rate system requires a supra-national framework for co-operation. Until such time, in the words of the Bundesbank deputy President, Hans Tietmeyer, 'the EMS applies, with fixed, but adjustable rates'.

The EMS is simply a system of rules which must be operated by the central banks within the Mechanism. The Maastricht Treaty made no formal changes to the rules, but did change the way in which they were being operated. It is rather like trying to fly in a sports car by driving it very fast over the edge of a cliff. There is nothing mechanically wrong with the car, it's just for driving in, not flying.

Conclusion

If the ERM is to operate as a system of 'permanently' fixed exchange rates it requires a new supra-national framework, such as a European Central Bank, for setting monetary policy. Countries which are unwilling to cede sovereignty to such an institution will realign their currencies from time to time.

EXPLANATION 3 — THE MARKETS ARE TOO POWERFUL WITH FREE CAPITAL FLOWS

The 1983 realignment of the French franc was accompanied by a whole package of measures to deal with the currency crisis. Among these, French tourists were allowed to purchase only

2,000 francs per adult per year for spending abroad while children had a 1,000 franc allowance. The French press looked forward to a summer of budget holidays abroad for French tourists surrounded by free-spending Germans and Americans. The ruling illustrates the extent to which the early ERM crises were managed with the assistance of capital flows. Given the magnitude of the speculative flows unleashed in mid-1992, European central bankers discussed re-introducing such controls. It appeared that the commitment to freeing restrictions on investment flows in Stage One of the Delors process, was threatening the stability of the European Monetary System as a whole, the central bank reserves swept aside by the billions of Deutschmarks in hot money flows.

In fact the evidence to support this thesis is rather mixed. Sterling and the lira were forced to quit the system in dramatic circumstances, but in the light of our earlier discussion the central banks were largely defending the indefensible. It was also not surprising that the mechanisms for central bank co-operation failed to work given the fact that the Bundesbank felt a realignment *was* necessary. Ironically, for all the talk of Bundesbank dominance in Europe, it was the weaker currency central bankers who initially won the day by forcing heavy pan-European intervention and a German rate cut. In contrast, the bout of speculation against the French franc was met with a joint Franco-German statement that a realignment was not required. The Bundesbank intervened within the ERM band rather than at the limit as required by EMS rules and sanctioned a further easing in monetary policy. Finally the DMark/French franc rate lifted off the ERM floor and the Exchange Rate Mechanism was preserved.

Reintroducing capital controls would certainly be a blow to European integration and economic development. The Spanish decision to tighten controls was immediately followed by a sharp rise in bond yields and falls in Spanish equities — developments which were only partially reversed when controls were lifted following the November devaluation. Inward investment flows are very much dependent on a company's ability to eventually repatriate profits. With capital controls the Exchange Rate Mechanism's role in encouraging economic convergence is also diluted. But the hot money flows are certainly reducing the flexibility of the authorities. As long as independent currencies and monetary policies exist they will be capable of ultimately forcing realignments. Given this the gradualist approach to monetary union outlined in the Maastricht Treaty (in which realignments become increasingly infrequent) looks increasingly unworkable. But if the System is throwing up the wrong policy outcomes anyway, perhaps this failure is desirable. It is to the symptoms of policy failure, and in particular high pan-European unemployment to which we now turn.

EXPLANATION 4 — HIGH UNEMPLOYMENT REFLECTS PROBLEMS WITH DOMESTIC ECONOMIES — NOT THE ERM!

The strongest argument that the ERM policy has created unnecessarily tight monetary policy hinges on mounting unemployment set against high real interest rates. The contrast between the EC experience of unemployment and that in the rest of the world is illustrated if we compare today's levels with those in 1980. At the beginning of the 1980s, the Community unemployment rate stood at 7 per cent, in line with that in the United States, but well above the 2 per cent rate in Japan. Twelve years later, there has been a two and a half percentage point increase in the pan-European unemployment rate, to just under 10 per cent, while US and Japanese rates are only very slightly higher. It is not just a question of the numbers out of work, but also the duration of unemployment. In the Community, over half of those out of work have been unemployed for more than a year, a development which not only has a high social cost but may also damage the labour force for the future.

For economists, the cause of unemployment can be viewed in several ways. Looking at the economy in aggregate, there may well be negative shocks which cause firms to reduce the number of employees, perhaps due to a sharp fall in a country's exports or a rise in taxes which depresses consumer demand. This approach led to Keynesian policies in the 1950s and 1960s, where governments largely concentrated on keeping demand at just the right level. But employment and hours worked can also be treated like any other commodity. If there is a surplus of workers leading to high unemployment, then the 'price of labour' should fall to bring demand and supply into line. This approach to unemployment concentrates on the individual decisions taken every day in the labour market — are firms reluctant to hire the unemployed? are those out of work actively seeking employment? are wages set to fall?

It may initially appear to be a failure of the ERM approach that the Banque de France was unable to ease monetary policy as French unemployment edged back above 10 per cent in early 1992. The system appears to have increased, not reduced, the cost of keeping down domestic inflation. However, it turns out that there is a considerable body of research pointing to detailed features of the European labour markets as the primary cause of persistent high unemployment. Open-ended welfare benefits, for example, can slow the search for a new job or make the unemployed unwilling to accept a wage cut. Those out of work may be keen to find employment but lack the appropriate skills. This approach suggests that government policy needs to be re-orientated to more 'active' policies for the unemployed, such as training and placement, rather than 'passive' policies of simply maintaining their income. The legislative framework for employment is also extremely important. An OECD analysis of the rise in European unemployment noted that it is primarily explained by a sharp drop in hiring, rather than redundancies. This reluctance to hire may in turn be traced to employee protection legislation and the non-wage costs (such as social security contributions) of a new employee.

The French case requires particular scrutiny as France has given up a large degree of policy independence within the ERM. The Mitterrand government took power in 1981 with an ambitious programme to tackle unemployment and of social reform. Its fiscal reflation package included measures to expand public sector employment and was planned to directly add $1\frac{3}{4}$ per cent to national output over the first two years. France was acting alone in following this expansionary course and widening trade deficits triggered heavy downward pressure on the franc. The franc's devaluation in mid-1982 was accompanied by measures to combat inflation and a further devaluation in March 1983 brought a major tightening of fiscal policy, a reduction in money supply targets and the restrictions on French tourists' purchases of other currencies. Unemployment had risen from $2\frac{1}{2}$ per cent in 1970 to $7\frac{1}{2}$ per cent in 1981, and following the Mitterrand U-turn the rate reached $10\frac{1}{2}$ per cent. Although France has accepted the discipline of the ERM and inflation has been reduced to just 3 per cent, the rate of unemployment has fallen little from this 1986/87 peak.

Growth in France between 1986 and 1990 averaged 3 per cent each year, but employment growth was very subdued. Employers were reluctant to hire, despite the level of unemployment. This suggests that the root of the problem may lie with the detailed performance of the labour market, not macro-economic policy. The national minimum wage (the SMIC) may prevent low-skilled workers from finding work, while non-wage costs for employers (such as social security contributions) add 40 per cent to basic wages and salaries. There is also evidence of a poor mis-match between the skills of the unemployed and the available vacancies. Prudent national economic policies may simply be revealing some of these underlying structural problems.

Conclusion

Unemployment in Europe is disturbingly high, but the solution may lie with domestic labour-market policies, not a revamp of European policy co-ordination.

CONCLUSIONS

Oscar Wilde's Algernon states that 'The truth is rarely pure and never simple. Modern life would be very tedious if it were either, and modern literature a complete impossibility!'.

This Chapter may leave the reader wanting to substitute 'economics' for 'literature'. The nature of the ERM crisis was determined by personalities and coincidence as well as economic fundamentals. But some general conclusions can be drawn:

Summary: the roots of the ERM crisis

- A major realignment was required for some currencies, particularly sterling. Policy shocks, primarily in Germany, contributed to pressure for rate adjustments and this is reflected in high real interest rates across Europe.

- The ERM cannot gradually develop into a fixed rate system, unless there is a major overhaul of the rules for co-ordination.
- Free capital flows reduce the flexibility of central banks to follow independent policies, but the re-introduction of controls would damage long-term growth prospects.
- The cause of high European unemployment lies as much with domestic labour markets as external policy failures.

It is clear that the Delors plan and its Maastricht Treaty counterpart are seriously flawed. In the run up to Stage Three and the establishment of a European Central Bank, EC countries cannot request a devaluation. De facto control over interest rates goes to the Bundesbank, where only the German States are represented. Given this flaw, the proposals for a small-scale currency union involving France, Germany and the Benelux countries with a new representative central bank are a logical and healthy step. The prospects for such a union and its implications for broader European integration are dealt with in the final chapter of this book.

Other EC countries are now set to reassess their individual roles in the pan-European programme to currency union. The benefits of a single currency (Chapter 4), the reasons for exchange rate adjustments (Chapter 5) and the relationship between national and European policy within the Single Currency Area (Chapter 6) are issues which each have an important place in this debate.

Part
TWO

··

THREE ISSUES IN THE ERM CONTROVERSY

··

Chapter
FOUR

A SINGLE MARKET, A SINGLE CURRENCY

••

A UNITED STATES OF EUROPE?

Against the backdrop of the recent ERM crisis, the goal of a single European currency appears to be very distant and fraught with difficulties. It is true that the development of a continent-wide ECU area represents a unique experiment for Europe. But there is concrete evidence that such federations can work — indeed the most successful, the United States of America, dominates world economic affairs. Does this provide a suitable blueprint for a 'United States of Europe'?

Fears that a pan-European monetary union would simply be too large and the member economies too diverse to be practical may be discounted by the North American experience. The United States is not only striking in size — a population of 250 million people — but it also spans immense regional diversity in terms of climate, natural resources, and production patterns. If we consider each of the American states as individual economies then we can trace wide disparities. Alaska depends on mineral extraction for one-third of state GNP, while financial services have a relatively minor role in the local economy. In contrast New York state has negligible natural resources but its powerful financial services industry contributes $102 bn, roughly 23 per cent, to the value of state output.

The use of the US dollar and the absence of state trade controls have contributed to the creation of a vast integrated market for goods and services. Take a minor consumer item such as the soap bar — annual sales are worth $1.5 bn and half this market is taken by just two major companies, Lever Brothers and Procter & Gamble. Faced with such a vast market these companies can exploit economies of scale in production, distribution and marketing and thus bring prices down sharply. It is not only the markets for final consumer products which have become continent-wide. The absence of state controls on migration within the United States has created a labour market of 200 million workers. With a single currency, salary and wage conditions are easily comparable and income earned in one state can be spent in another without fears of currency fluctuations.

The American experience also demonstrates that widely divergent economic fortunes are consistent with a single currency. Individual states are hit by positive and negative economic shocks, such as an oil price jump, a boom in financial services or technological innovation in the computer industry. Adjustments to dollar interest rates by the US central bank in Washington or Congressional debates on the budget deficit may appear remote to the average Texan, but the pressures for 'opting out' are very muted or indeed non-existent. The economic dislocation associated with the creation of a 'Texan dollar', or a currency for the whole of the American South-West, would be profound.

Certainly the standard of living enjoyed by the average citizen of this economic confederation is relatively high. Recent data show that the GNP (a measure of national output) per head in west Germany is only 75 per cent of that in the United States. In the poorest EC country, Greece, GNP per head is only 35 per cent of the American figure. US prosperity naturally reflects a number of factors, such as its endowment of natural resources, but it may have been enhanced by the dollar's role as a continent-wide currency. The ECU enthusiasts turn to the US and say they have seen the future for Europe — and it works.

LEVELS OF INTEGRATION

How then do we get from the national economies to a vast integrated European economy on the same scale as the United States? We can break down the measures into a series of steps:

- Remove tariff barriers, quotas and other limits to free trade.
- Harmonise market rules and regulations (eg. safety testing).
- Allow free movement of people and capital between economies.
- Stabilise exchange rates.
- Introduce a single currency.

The convincing arguments for opening up domestic markets to European competition have long been recognised by the 12 EC Governments. The Single European Act, signed in February 1986, set the objective of creating a unified internal market for Europe by the end of 1992. While European trade agreements had in the past largely been concerned with removing tariffs and quota restrictions, the Single European Act has gone much further than that. Technical barriers (such as governmental regulations) must be swept away and tax rates harmonised to allow fair competition. The full implementation of the Act will create highly competitive pan-European markets dwarfing even those in the United States.

The 1988 Cecchini Report set out to quantify the economic benefits from European economic integration. The exploitation of economies of scale and improved allocation of resources due to enhanced market competition would add 2 per cent directly to EC output, according to the report. It argues that these supply-side effects would also simplify economic management by governments (by reducing inflation, for example), and that as a result the total GNP increase would be around 6 per cent. The total employment gain across Europe due to the implementation of the Single Act was put at 1.8 million.

But it is not inevitable that close economic integration will be followed by monetary union — Canada signed a free trade agreement with the United States in January 1988 but is not under pressure to abandon the Canadian dollar. Indeed, distinguished economists opposed to monetary union (such as Martin Feldstein) strongly support the economic integration which removal of barriers to trade and mobility will bring. They favour Stage One of the Maastricht timetable which, in removing limits on free capital flows, contributes to the improved efficiency of the financial markets. But they argue that artificially stabilising exchange rates and ultimately embracing monetary union is a separate step, involving uncertain benefits and creating problems of economic management.

For the individual businessman signing an export contract, the ERM represents an improvement as it offers relative currency stability. For the tourist at the bureau de change, the ability to spend ECUs both at home and on holiday abroad will be welcome. These direct benefits of the steps to monetary union will be evaluated in this chapter, while the problems this presents for policy makers will be evaluated in a later chapter.

STABLE CURRENCIES

The financial pages of the national newspapers often carry reports dramatising developments on the foreign exchange markets: 'the Italian lira slumped to a 5-year low' or 'the dollar soared on stronger US retail sales data'. That the ERM has been successful in dampening this currency volatility can be clearly seen from Figure 4.1, showing how the German mark

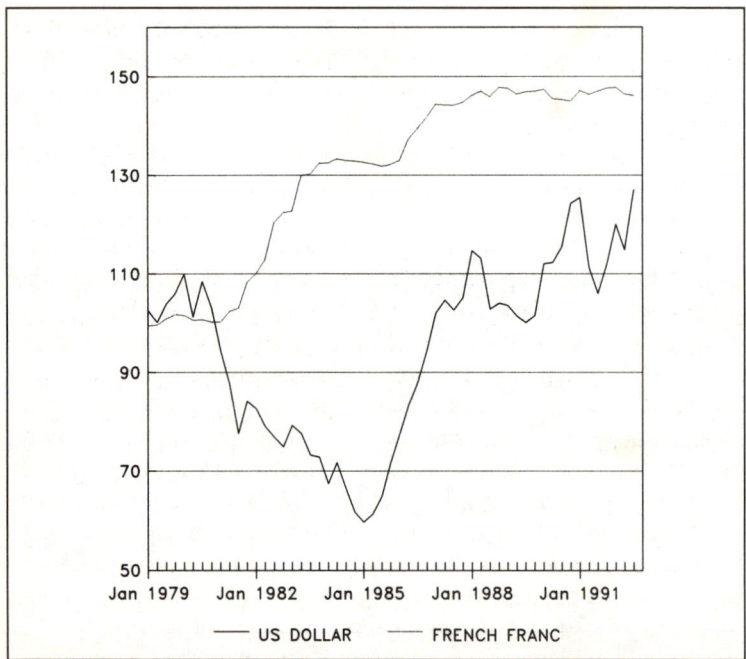

Figure 4.1 DMark value against US$ and French franc (First Quarter 1979 = 100)

has moved against the French franc and the US dollar since the ERM was established in 1979. Over this period there has been a trend appreciation of the DM against both currencies; indeed, the French franc has depreciated by close to 50 per cent over that period through successive ERM realignments. However, the franc has become progressively more stable through the 1980s and since the last devaluation, in 1987, has traded within a $4\frac{1}{2}$ per cent range. In contrast, the dollar's movements have been characterised both by greater month-to-month volatility and sustained swings away from the underlying trend which have ultimately been reversed. The Deutschmark's purchasing power against the US dollar had almost been halved by the second quarter of 1985 (when \$1 bought DM 3.31) but rebounds sharply over the next seven years (\$1 eventually buys only DM 1.62).

Exporter's profitability

For the company heavily involved in international trade, this exchange rate volatility is reflected in uncertain and erratic profitability. Consider the relative fortunes of two car exporters to the German market, one with its production facilities located in France, the other in the United States. The impact of the exchange rate changes on a measure of profitability for each exporter is outlined in the box. As a simplifying assumption, suppose Deutschmark car prices rise exactly in line with German inflation, and production costs increase with domestic inflation (in France and the United States). Figure 4.2 illustrates how over the 1980s the French producer's profitability dips in the mid 1980s, but even at the low-point this exporter is making a modest profit. In contrast, the US producer's competitive advantage in 1979, gives way to a substantial loss per car in early 1985. The reason for this is relatively straightforward to pin down. Over this period US costs have gone up by 50 per cent but DMark revenues have risen by only 30 per cent, reflecting the difference in inflation rates. The DMark, pushed well away from its true underlying value by market forces, has failed to reflect this inflation differential — indeed, the DMark has weakened sharply. By 1992, the United States producer's original profitability has been restored but the fact that the pronounced swings in profitability can have a powerful impact on trade flows

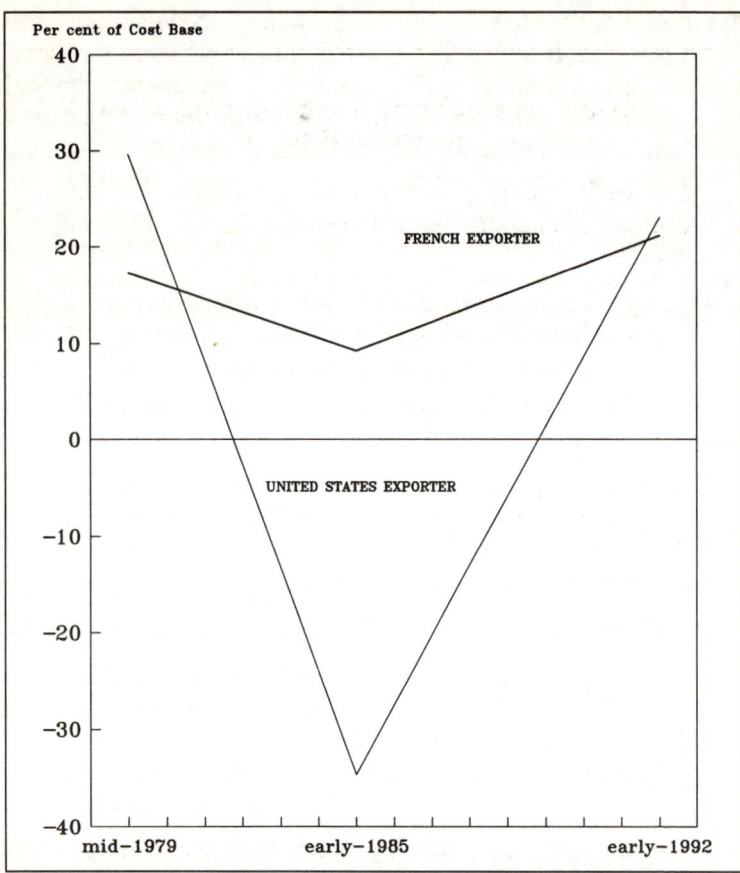

Figure 4.2 Profitability for exporters to Germany
Illustrative figures — based on CPI/exchange rate data

is borne out by the statistics. General Motor's North American exports to Western Europe fell from 24,400 vehicles in 1980, to 1,103 in 1985, before rebounding to 17,500 in 1991.

If currency movements were largely predictable or simply reflected inflation differentials then their impact on trade would be contained. But given the exchange rate volatility evident in freely floating markets over the past decade, a company operating outside the ERM is likely to be wary of becoming too heavily dependent on export earnings or imported inputs. When it spots the opportunity to compete effectively in a foreign market, it is

Impact of exchange rate changes on profitability

For each exporter to the German market, we can express profitability as a percentage in the following manner:

> DMark car price *less* DMark distribution cost
> Converted into home currency
> *less* Domestic costs in home currency
>
> Expressed as a percentage of domestic costs in home currency

As this is a percentage measure we can compare the profitability per car of the two exporters in the light of the exchange rate developments. What influences this profitability? For the US producer:

Profit calculation	*Influence (and direction)*
DMark car price	General car prices (+)
	German inflation (+)
Conversion into US$s	DM's value against $ (+)
Domestic costs	General cost of labour (−)
	United States inflation (−)

If German inflation is much slower than US inflation, then there is a potential problem for the US exporter to Germany. Hopefully the DMark will appreciate against the dollar to make allowances for this inflation differential. In economists' jargon if the DMark appreciates by just the right amount to offset the inflation differential then the 'real exchange rate' is unchanged. If the DMark falls rather than rises (as we see from Figure 4.1) then its 'real exchange rate' is much lower, and the US exporter won't operate as profitably in the German markets. Similar arguments can be made for the French franc and its export industry.

likely to hesitate on the grounds that any competitive advantage may quickly be erased by a currency appreciation. Certainly where a large investment is required, in plant or equipment or distribution, the required rate of return will be higher to reflect the increased uncertainty. Our American car exporter may decide to produce in Europe, where, although there aren't the same economies of scale as in North America, it will be less exposed to the 'roulette' of the foreign exchange markets. As a result, exchange rate variability may impede economic efficiency and lower living standards for all countries involved in international trade. The ERM can be viewed as giving *free* insurance, protecting the company against adverse exchange rate changes.

Managing currency exposure

These arguments suggest that a stable currency framework, such as the ERM, is a prerequisite for successful economic integration. But there are free trade areas, such as that in North America where industries appear to have overcome the problems associated with volatile exchange rates — Canada takes nearly a quarter of US exports while the United States accounts for over three-fifths of Canadian exports. Economists have several explanations for this. Major corporations employ sophisticated treasury departments to manage their currency exposure, often turning to the forward markets to convert future receipts into their home currency. The forward markets give the value of one currency in terms of another at some future date, so in early 1979 the US exporter could have sold the projected DMark revenues in 1985 and bought dollars to cover the 1985 costs. The currency market's quotation for this transaction depends on interest rate differentials. Dollar rates were higher than those in Deutschmarks in 1979, and the market was expecting a DMark appreciation to make the dollar and DMarks equally attractive investments. As Figure 4.3 shows, using the forward markets the US exporter could have locked in its 1985 operating profits. Even if the company was not sure of its exact 1985 revenues it could hedge the bulk of its exposure and fine-tune the rest closer to the time. Companies with international exposure may also fund their investments by borrowing abroad so that the capital cost of a plant is fixed in foreign currency terms. Future foreign currency receipts thus match future debt payments.

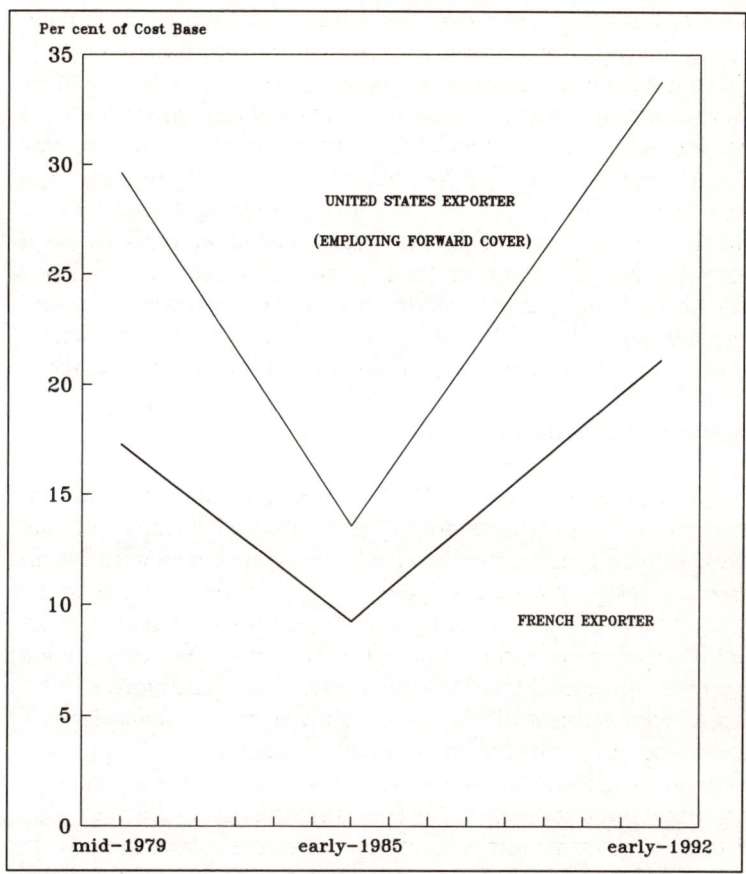

Figure 4.3 US exporter employs forward cover

A more subtle argument focuses on the way in which currency volatility is linked to other types of risk in the economic environment. Suppose that our car exporters are among many such manufacturers in France and the United States — cars dominate exports for both countries. These exporters are vulnerable to a sudden shift in foreign demand away from their product as well as Deutschmark volatility. But the two risks are related — if there is a 20 per cent drop in the price of cars due to a sudden weakening in demand, then the dollar may come under downward pressure given the importance of cars for the US balance of payments. Figure 4.4 shows profit projections for

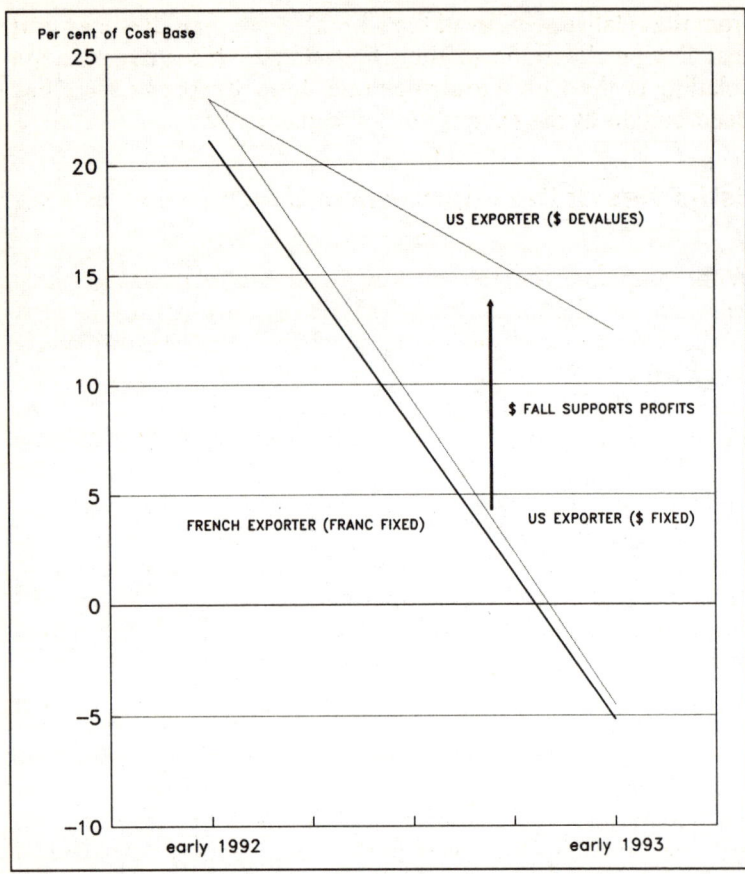

Figure 4.4   Profitability and currency adjustment

the two exporters in the first quarter of 1993 on the assumption that the dollar weakens leaving the DMark 15 per cent stronger in dollar terms. Anchored within the ERM, the franc cannot adjust to a lower level, indeed, Banque de France efforts to support the currency through higher interest rates may deepen the misery of the French exporter. Exchange rate adjustments may thus act as a protective buffer for exporters, encouraging specialisation in foreign trade rather than impeding it.

There is a final fly in the ERM ointment and that hinges on the fact that we are not stabilising all currency rates here, only those in Europe. It is true that the French exporters will benefit from the relative stability of the FFr/DM rate, but they may find that linking the franc to the Deutschmark has increased the volatility of the FFr/$ exchange rate. Intra-European trade has been bought at the expense of transatlantic trade.

Estimates of the importance of stable currencies

With competing theories on how much stable exchange rates will add to European living standards, turning to detailed mathematical models of international trade may help quantify these gains. The failure of the post-war fixed exchange rate system in 1973 led to an abrupt increase in currency gyrations, and a good opportunity to study their impact on trade. A decade later the International Monetary Fund published a major review which came to the rather surprising conclusion that: 'The large majority of empirical studies ... are unable to establish a systematically significant link between measured exchange rate variability and the volume of international trade'. Three studies did manage to identify a relationship between the two but they were based on rather unusual circumstances or methods of analysis.

These statistical-based models have their limitations, however, and their critics argue that instead of asking economists about currency instability we should ask those affected, the businesspeople. Recent polls of European businesspeople, including a major CBI survey in the UK, suggest that exchange rate stability helps companies plan for the future and is seen as an important benefit of the ERM.

Certainly, trade within Europe has been prospering since the Exchange Rate Mechanism was put in place. Germany's imports from France expanded by 78 per cent in the 1980s, almost double the growth rate of imports from the United States. Unfortunately, the contribution which currency stability alone has played in promoting this trade remains rather clouded in mystery. On balance, it is likely that reduced exchange rate variability does reduce uncertainty and thus ultimately improves economic efficiency. However, the impact on living standards are probably very modest, perhaps of the order of $\frac{1}{2}$ per cent of annual output.

ADOPTING THE ECU

It is often argued that the greatest gains from monetary union come with the final stage — the adoption of the ECU as a single European currency. Certainly the advantages are more readily identified, as anyone arriving late at night at a provincial Italian airport with a wallet full of Deutschmarks will readily testify.

The currency conversion industry within Europe is well-established — from the high street bureau de change to the foreign exchange dealer on an international bank's trading floor. The costs for the individual business traveller or tourist appear to be the highest. The Bureau Européen des Unions de Consomateurs (BEUC) in 1988 conducted an experiment which rather neatly demonstrates how these costs mount up. A businessman sets out from Brussels with 40,000 Belgian francs and in turn visits each of the Community capitals (excluding Luxembourg and Dublin). At each step banknotes are converted into the local currency, and by the end of the journey transaction costs have reduced the original sum to only 21,300 francs — a loss of 47 per cent. The greatest losses were in the weakest currencies, such as the drachma, while the average cost of banknote conversion was around $2\frac{1}{2}$ per cent. Has the stability associated with the ERM improved this situation? Table 4.1 shows a selection of buy and sell rates for foreign banknotes quoted on London's Oxford Street in mid-1992 (this may introduce a welcome piece of nostalgia for British tourists). The evidence suggests that the buy-sell spreads remained relatively wide, averaging just over 7 per cent, despite sterling's membership of the Mechanism. It is a measure of the distortions created by this system that a major UK tour operator providing bureau de change services is concentrating on this part of its business since it has proved consistently more profitable.

Survey evidence from the European Commission indicates that the cost of foreign currency transactions is closely related to the size of the transaction. At around ECU 100,000 the cost is roughly 0.5 per cent, dropping to 0.3 per cent for amounts over ECU 5 million. Relating these estimates to the revenues of the banking system it appears that direct savings from adopting the ECU would be around one-fifth of one per cent of total output — ECU 11 million per year. But note that this is based on existing levels of international business, and that

Table 4.1 Bureau de change buy and sell rates in London, mid-1992

Foreign currency banknotes	Bought at	Sold at	Spread (%)
Deutschmark	2.97	2.77	7.2
Spanish peseta	188	175	7.4
French franc	10.00	9.33	7.2
Danish krone	11.45	10.67	7.3

as European integration deepens these savings will become increasingly important. Countries such as Portugal, where the escudo is not widely used in international business and the banking system is relatively unsophisticated, will be the biggest beneficiaries. This analysis concentrates on the external costs of single currencies, but there are also savings within companies when large treasury departments are trimmed. So far the ECU has been little used in commerce, in invoicing or transfer pricing, as this is regarded by finance directors as simply adding an additional layer of complexity. Companies such as Airbus Industrie, the multinational consortium constructing aeroplanes, which might appear to have much to gain by using the ECU, are still invoicing in dollars. It seems that only with the formal adoption of the ECU as a single currency will corporations reap the full benefits from simplifying accounting and planning procedures.

In contrast to its limited commercial use, the ECU's role in the debt markets is increasingly important. European governments and companies are choosing to issue bonds denominated in ECUs, rather than in their home currency and the ECU bond market has grown from ECU 280 million in 1981 to ECU 14,081 million in 1991. Governments may be able to borrow at lower interest rates in the ECU market as they no longer have the option of devaluing their currencies and thus reducing the value of their debt in hard currency terms. Ultimately national currency markets will be replaced by a single international ECU bond market, comparable in size to the United States Treasury market. Such a market will be more efficient both for borrowers and investors in Europe, and will encourage overseas financial institutions to invest in Europe.

Market researchers and forward-looking advertising executives talk about 'the European market' but, in reality, it remains a series of fragmented national markets. There are wide price differentials for similar goods and services throughout the EC and even in Northern Europe where living standards are roughly similar. The price of a car before tax may be 45 per cent higher in England than in Luxembourg. Using a single currency for pricing may well ease price comparisons across Europe and encourage international trade. Economists refer to this as 'price transparency'. With *Liberation*, the French newspaper, costing 85p in London, 6 francs in Paris and 2,200 lira in Milan, it takes a calculator to discover where it is cheapest. In the case of a newspaper this is merely a matter of interest. For a manufacturer choosing suppliers from anywhere in the EC market, the use of a single currency will mean one fewer impediment to international trade and complement the 1992 process.

Set against the welfare gains from economic integration, the advantages of a single currency appear to be on a much smaller scale. While the Cecchini Report concludes that the 1992 Community market could add as much as 7.7 per cent to Community GNP, the analysis of monetary union so far has identified much smaller gains. The European Commission report on European monetary union argues that this is because the analysis has been static rather than 'dynamic'. It is static because it looks at Europe at one point in time and asks how much better off would we be with monetary union? But a single currency will put us on a completely different *growth path* and in the long run European output may be 5 to 10 per cent higher than in the case where we retain our national currencies.

This argument hinges on the impact of monetary union on the uncertainty which companies face in planning for the future. If they face a high degree of uncertainty then the required return from any investment in plant or equipment or research, for example, will be greater. Monetary union, in sweeping away exchange rate volatility and reducing the risk of a national economic policy shock, helps companies plan with a greater degree of certainty. As a result investment is promoted and each year growth is slightly faster as a result. Only a $\frac{1}{2}$ per cent fall in the required rate of return on investment will add 5 to 10 per cent to European living standards in the long run. This argument is attractive but depends on two critical assumptions. Firstly, that in anchoring exchange rates uncertainty is reduced rather than simply moved to other economic variables (such as interest rates or house prices). Secondly, that overall economic policy, including taxes and public spending, will be more stable in a single-currency Europe. Each of these assumptions must be examined critically.

SUMMARY: A SINGLE MARKET, A SINGLE CURRENCY

- The United States with its single currency and absence of trade barriers is in many ways a blue-print for European integration. Vast and highly competitive markets have helped Americans achieve a high standard of living.
- The removal of barriers to trade and mobility in Europe will bring important gains in economic welfare, but the ERM and monetary union represent separate steps with their own benefits and costs.
- The ERM framework for stability in exchange rates reduces uncertainty and may promote intra-European trade, but many expert studies cast doubt on the magnitude of this improvement.
- The *direct* gains of a single currency, such as the elimination of conversion costs, are readily identifiable and will become steadily more important with greater economic integration.
- The long-term gains from the certainties of a single currency may be the most important, but must be studied in a broader economic context which addresses the question: why do currencies adjust?

Chapter
FIVE

THE CASE FOR CURRENCY ADJUSTMENTS

●●●

CURRENCY STABILITY — AT WHAT COST?

Stable exchange rates may be desirable for the company heavily involved in international trade. But perhaps this holds true for other prices set in free markets. Rather than allowing the relative price of gold and silver to swing around, reflecting demand and supply influences, why not help consumers by fixing them too? A European Precious Metals Mechanism could be set up with large scale official intervention if gold and silver prices get out of line. This doesn't happen because it is recognised in a market economy that a price acts as a signal — a price rise dampening demand and helping to boost production. Economists generally agree on one thing — that changes in prices are a symptom of the underlying shocks to the economic system and not by themselves a harmful source of variability. A strike at a South African gold mine may boost the gold price; government action to resolve the strike is required, not a ceiling on the gold price. It is a commitment to the allocation of resources through free competitive markets which has helped Western economies reach a standard of living well above that in the planned economies of Eastern Europe.

Similar issues must be considered in assessing whether exchange rates should change. If the Italian lira loses ground against the Deutschmark perhaps that change is acting as a signal that the Italian economy must be more competitive relative to Germany, and the resulting Italian export gains actually contribute to overall economic stability. Attempts to maintain the currency within an artificial strait-jacket might well create strains and problems in other markets, particularly in related financial markets. Following the Italian elections in April 1992, there was an international crisis of confidence in the Italian economy as politicians struggled vainly to agree on a new President and government. Just before the appointment of Giuliano Amato as prime minister the lira/DM exchange rate peaked at 762 lira, compared with 755 earlier in the year. Was this minor 1 per cent depreciation a testimony to the ERM's ability to reduce uncertainty? The currency was stable, but at the cost of interest rate instability. Three-month interest rates rose sharply, from 12 per cent to 17 per cent in just three months as the Bank of Italy battled to underpin confidence in the lira.

Speculative upward pressure on a currency can be as much a problem for policy-makers as this Italian crisis. For the United Kingdom, the decision by the Chancellor, Nigel Lawson, to link sterling to the Deutschmark in late 1987 had wide-ranging repercussions. Structural changes during the 1980s had laid the basis for a marked improvement in confidence among business people and consumers, and domestic demand growth accelerated strongly. In the first quarter of 1988 sterling remained under heavy upward pressure and despite heavy Bank of England intervention the 3.00 DM ceiling finally gave way in early March. The Chancellor's attempt at 'bucking the market' had failed, despite intervention totalling $10 bn. However, sterling's appreciation did ultimately prove unsustainable and by end-1989 it had drifted down to 2.80 DM in response to disappointing trade figures.

From one perspective the UK government had contributed to exchange rate stability, dampening a sterling surge which was unjustified and thus helping UK exporters retain markets share. But currency volatility had simply been traded for instability elsewhere in the economy. To contain sterling's gains, base rates in the United Kingdom were cut to $7\frac{1}{2}$ per cent in May 1988 despite clear evidence of overheating in domestic demand. Reflecting this monetary easing, money supply growth soared from $10\frac{1}{2}$ per cent at the end of 1987 to $17\frac{1}{2}$ per cent in the second half of 1988. While sterling was relatively stable, other asset prices rose sharply. House prices rose by a quarter in 1988, having increased by 15 per cent over each of the previous two years. Alan Walters, the distinguished British economist, argues that on that occasion 'joining the ERM club actually caused the monetary explosion'.

The Italian and United Kingdom examples illustrate that stabilising one financial variable can create instability elsewhere in the economy, particularly in other asset markets. But to understand why currencies will inevitably press against the constraints created by the ERM bands, we need to know what is forcing exchange rates to change. While the value of currency, like a commodity price, does match supply and demand, assessing how these arise is quite tricky. The good news is that we have 200 years of economic theory on which to draw. . . .

WHY DO EXCHANGE RATES START TO MOVE?

The currency markets simply bring together supply and demand for a currency. When the French franc/Deutschmark rate is quoted at 3.3645 this is the market price of the Deutschmark expressed in terms of the franc. Factors boosting demand for Deutschmarks will raise this price, factors reducing demand lower it. At some rate demand and supply are brought into equilibrium. Let us begin by reviewing the direct participants in the foreign exchange markets and understand how a change in the exchange rate promotes economic adjustment.

Trade flows

Clearly trade flows between countries create demand and supply for a currency. German exporters to France may well receive French francs initially but they then have to convert them back into Deutschmarks in order to meet their domestic costs. In contrast, French exporters to Germany sell Deutschmarks to repatriate their receipts from sales in Germany. If Germany's exports exceeds its imports — a trade surplus — then there is net demand for Deutschmarks due to trade flows. How does an exchange rate appreciation help correct this situation? As the Deutschmark appreciates initially this may exacerbate the trade surplus, but over time Germany's exporting sector will become increasingly uncompetitive. Ultimately the German export sector will be unable to export profitably to France, while there is a corresponding improvement in the fortunes of French exporters. Eventually the trade imbalance is likely to be corrected.

If we start with trade equilibrium, then an economic shock, say a sharp oil price rise due to a supply interruption, will have a different impact on different countries' trade positions. Germany is dependent on overseas sources for all its oil consumption, while Norway in contrast has a net surplus on its oil account. A sharp increase in oil prices will boost the Norwegian krone at the expense of the DMark, making German exports increasingly competitive. It is true that Germany could become equally competitive through a national 20 per cent wage cut, but such a step would be painful and rather slow as wages tend to be rather slow to adjust. In economists' jargon they are known as 'sticky' prices.

Asset allocation

Financial flows between currencies are also creating flows in the foreign exchange markets. A German resident holding an equity stake in a French company will receive French franc dividends which are then converted back into Deutschmarks. In the short-term money markets, the German investor may believe that French franc interest rates are relatively attractive. If the additional return offsets the risk of a French franc devaluation, he may well reallocate his portfolio in favour of the franc.

An economic shock will no doubt influence asset allocation as well as trade flows. If there is a political crisis such as that in Italy during the summer of 1992, foreign investors lose confidence in the outlook for the Italian economy and require a higher return from Italian money market assets. The expected return from holding assets is made up of two elements: any lira appreciation (or depreciation) against the investors' home currency and the interest rate on lira deposits. If the exchange rate falls sharply, indeed overshoots its true long-term equilibrium value, then eventually the prospect of a currency rebound will keep investors holding lira. It is true that sharply increasing lira interest rates will prevent an outflow of capital from Italy, but they may be much more damaging to the Italian economy than any temporary currency weakness.

This discussion suggests that exchange rate fluctuations, rather than being harmful, can actually encourage economic stability. The jumps in currency values dramatised in the daily press are not a sign of instability but appropriate, as other relative prices (such as wages) can be 'sticky'. However, a currency devaluation may appear to help economic policy-makers in the short-term, only to create second-round effects which undermine long-term economic stability. Anxiety over the long-run impact of exchange rate adjustments, plays an important role in support for the Exchange Rate Mechanism.

Ultimately the supply of Deutschmarks is not controlled by exporters, importers or financial institutions; it is the Bundesbank which prints the notes and will restrict Deutschmark supply if its value falls sharply. The long-term value of a currency can eventually be traced back to monetary policy in the country concerned. Economists use a theory of 'purchasing power parity' to explain currency trends over decades. The theory argues that in the long run exchange rates adjust so that purchasers are indifferent to buying traded goods in their home country, or buying from abroad after converting their currency. So:

Price of goods in France (francs)
= Price of goods in Germany (DM) × FFr-DM rate

If inflation is 5 per cent in France and 3 per cent in Germany then the franc will depreciate by 2 per cent each year on trend. Indeed, the external value of a currency may play an important part in the way interest rates influence the economy. If policy is tightened by raising interest rates, then the currency will appreciate and thus help to put downward pressure on domestic input costs and wages.

Let us return to the two main reasons for undertaking transactions in the currency markets — trade and asset allocation — and understand why exchange rate fluctuations can be an indication of unhealthy long-term policy developments rather than simply contributing to short-term economic stability.

Trade flows revisited

Take the case of Norway and Germany outlined above and ask: what happens to domestic wages and prices in Germany as the DMark depreciates? If the answer is nothing, that's fine, there has been a real adjustment in the currency and Germany will have a competitive advantage in non-oil goods. But suppose the sharp rise in oil prices reinforced by the currency depreciation leads to a sharp rise in input prices. If the Bundesbank does nothing to counteract this pick-up in inflation then before long higher costs will be reflected in output price increases, and Germany will lose its competitive advantage. The United Kingdom's successive sterling devaluations in the 1960s and 1970s failed to lead to a sustained improvement in UK competitiveness. Indeed, an analysis by Professors Artis and Currie indicates that the competitive advantage from a devaluation was washed away by domestic inflation within five years. The only net result is higher UK prices.

Asset allocation revisited

In the context of the Italian political crisis, allowing the lira to depreciate may undermine confidence in the authorities to a greater degree. Rather than as a short-term pressure valve the currency weakness becomes chronic and a more profound currency crisis develops. Arguably a sharp increase in interest rates would force the politicians to solve the underlying problem. Allowing the currency to depreciate simply represents a short-term expedient and delays a long-term solution.

The distinction between temporary currency adjustments and long-term trends is critical in the ERM debate. Volatility in a country's real exchange rate, ie creating a sustained improvement or deterioration in its industries' competitiveness, can have a place in encouraging short-term adjustments. Those currently calling for a devaluation of the French franc against the DMark argue such a move would not boost domestic inflation, which at $2\frac{1}{2}$ per cent is well under control, and would facilitate a cut in French rates. Indeed, the United States was successful in devaluing the dollar in 1991/1992, without significantly adding to inflationary pressures while short-term interest rates have been cut to just 3 per cent.

During the 1980s the dollar displayed two clear 'trend' moves (see Chapter 4): an appreciation through to mid-1985, followed by a depreciation. A school of financial market analysts argue that while economists like to think of currencies in theoretical terms, speculative pressures dominate in practice and speculators make money backing trends. There is increasing evidence of currency 'bandwagons,' (trend moves without economic justification), but the policy response to this should be frequent central bank intervention as if the private sector behaviour is sub-optimal in the long-run the central banks should be able to beat the market. The answer is not to fix currencies within an inflexible grid.

In conclusion, there are circumstances in which exchange rate changes do have a role in promoting economic adjustment and something *is* lost in adopting a single currency for the whole EC area. To assess this cost we need to understand how frequent economic shocks are likely to be and the extent to which they will cause damaging economic divergences within the EC.

COUNTRY SHOCKS AND WHAT CHANGES IF EXCHANGE RATES ARE FIXED

The extent to which external shocks will create economic imbalances within the European Community depends primarily on the differences between member countries' economic structures. The greater the similarity between participating countries, then the more subdued will be the pressures to realign currencies in response to economic disturbances. Indeed, in the 1960s and 1970s, economists argued that there were some 'optimal' currency areas which could be identified by grouping together similar countries. Do the EC countries satisfy this requirement? Unfortunately there is no single measure of economic structure, just as there are many types of economic shock. Parameters which need to be considered include the general level of economic development, the natural resources in each country and the degree to which national industries have become specialised in certain product areas. A cursory survey indicates that structural differences within the EC are pronounced, a disparity which has been exacerbated by the community's expansion southward. There are marked differences in the standard of living throughout the Community (illustrated in Figure 5.1), well in excess of the disparities between individual states in the US. These stages of development are reflected in patterns of output; while on average only 7 per cent of the EC workforce is employed in agriculture, a quarter of Greek employment is in this sector. Economic dissimilarities are not

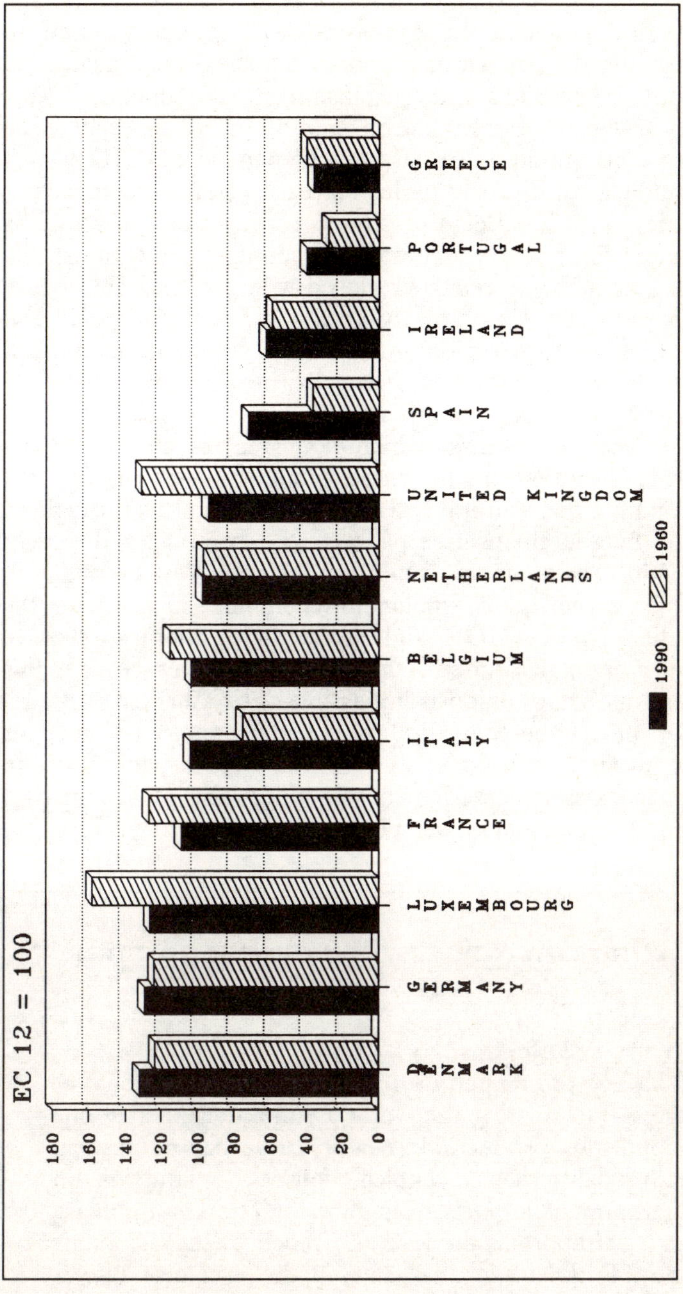

EC 12 = 100

Figure 5.1 Standard of living in EC member states

confined to the north–south divide. The oil price shocks in 1973 and 1979 demonstrated the importance of natural resources in determining the pattern of economic adjustments. The United Kingdom is running a trade surplus on energy products, but the EC as a whole is dependent on imports for 40 per cent of its energy consumption. An external demand shock, such as a sharp downturn in world trade, will have its greatest impact on countries such as Belgium where 16 per cent of GNP is accounted for by trade with non-EC countries. In contrast, the Spanish economy is relatively closed with a comparable figure of 5.5 per cent. Economic integration within Europe is also likely to encourage regions to specialise in the production of specific industrial products. Ironically, because of this special-isation, the success of economic union may increase the likeli-hood of economic shocks which would, in the absence of the ERM, create pressures for currency adjustments. Finally, it is worth noting that cultural and historical differences throughout Europe may in themselves prove fertile ground for divergent economic developments. While France and West Germany in 1989 appeared quite similar in economic structure – the revolution in the GDR and subsequent reunification have created a dramatic change in their relative fortunes. None of this suggests monetary union is impossible. The Chapter 3 discus-sion of the United States indicates that monetary union spans highly dissimilar regional economies. But if pan-European exchange rates are fixed then something else must adjust to realign competitiveness (see box).

What can adjust when exchange rates are fixed?

Wage adjustments
The key to competitiveness lies in the real exchange rate — to simplify the world assume there is just one input into production, labour, and that a German industrialist has a choice between production in Germany or imports from France. The Deutschmark cost of imports is the level of French wages divided by the FFr/DM exchange rate. If the exchange rate is

fixed then imports can only be made more competitive by a fall in French wages.

But how efficiently will this adjustment occur? It is clear that currency rates are extremely flexible, while research using mathematical models of European economies suggests that wages are rather 'sticky'. Only in the long run do wages display the necessary flexibility — and as Keynes pointed out, in the long run we are dead. In the short run it may require a period of high unemployment before the adjustment is finally complete. The cost over this period is in lost production and naturally the human cost associated with such lay-offs. Within single currency areas such as the United States, wages do adjust to reflect the relative economic fortunes of different regions — between 1983 and 1989, wages rose by a total of 10 per cent more in the north-east than in the west — but the process is comparatively languid.

People adjustment

Norman Tebbit, the British conservative politician, suggested that rather than rioting, the unemployed youth should get on their bikes and look for work. Within a single pan-European area workers may well be forced to take a plane in order to find employment. Economists refer to 'labour mobility' as a way in which economic adjustments can occur. Unfortunately, there is a strong cultural aversion in Europe to labour mobility — indeed, high unemployment rates in southern Italy and western France have not triggered mass labour migration. Over and above this, there are linguistic barriers for much of the current labour force. Labour mobility is unlikely to speed economic adjustments, indeed emigration may, as in the case of Ireland, reinforce regional economic under-performance.

Budgetary adjustment

Over the short-term, the only panacea with the currency fixed and monetary policy determined by a European central bank, may lie with fiscal policy — public spending and taxation in the region. A pan-European fiscal policy would adjust public spending and taxes to help depressed areas overcome negative economic shocks at the expense of their more prosperous neighbours, just as national governments do today. The interplay between national and pan-European fiscal policy is discussed in greater detail in Chapter 6. The European dimension of fiscal policy remains at a rather nebulous stage — expenditure in the General Community budget accounts for only 1 per cent of total GDP, in contrast to 15 per cent in the United States. Fixing national monetary policies and currency rates within the ERM without establishing a redistribution mechanism for European spending and tax revenues may be fraught with danger.

TWO CASE STUDIES — BRETTON WOODS AND THE 'SNAKE IN THE TUNNEL'

Over the past 50 years we have had a great deal of experience in pegging exchange rates, and perhaps the most valuable lessons lie in the failure of two systems — Bretton Woods in 1973 and the European 'Snake' during the 1970s. As the economic fortunes of member countries diverge, pressures for currencies to adjust grow and weaknesses in international co-ordination are exposed. The ERM and Maastricht frameworks have avoided some of the mistakes of these earlier pegged exchange rate regimes, but these two case studies demonstrate their vulnerability once market confidence is undermined.

Why Bretton Woods collapsed

In contrast to the ERM, at the centre of the Bretton Woods system lay a single currency, the dollar. Each country announced a fixed exchange rate for its currency against the dollar, and the central bank was compelled to intervene to defend this parity rate (within 1 per cent). In turn, the US agreed to convert dollars into gold at a fixed price, $35 an ounce. The system was thus a modified version of the inter-war Gold Standard. If a central bank ran into problems defending the parity rate, it could turn to the International Monetary Fund for loans. If it was clear that a long-term problem had arisen, then the dollar rate could be adjusted to reflect the 'fundamental disequilibrium'. It was the hope of the Bretton Woods architects that realignments would be infrequent, and despite the enormous economic change of the post-war years parity changes were indeed rare. However, the long stretches of stability illustrated in Figure 5.2, give a rather misleading indication of the stability of the system. Currency convertibility (into dollars) was only reintroduced in Europe in 1959, and central banks maintained tight controls on international capital flows. Thus fixed exchange rates were 'bought' at the expense of inefficient financial markets.

In the mid-1960s, the United States adopted expansionary policies — expanding spending on the Vietnam war and domestic programmes — and inflation began to accelerate. The link between the market price of gold and the dollar was broken in 1968. Unprecedented current account deficits also undermined market confidence in the US currency, and the European central banks were forced to intervene heavily. In 1971, the Smithsonian Agreement allowed a general dollar devaluation of 8 per cent, but heavy market speculation against the dollar forced a further devaluation of 10 per cent in early 1973. In a dramatic move, the foreign exchange markets were closed in March of that year, and when the markets reopened the dollar was floating.

The ERM does not have a single national currency at its heart, and thus is less vulnerable to policy developments in a single country. The 'divergence indicator', which measures a currency's deviation from its ECU central rate, shows whether policy in a particular country is out of line with the rest of Europe. The Bretton Woods case also illustrates that at the heart of any system of pegged exchange rates there must be a reasonable degree of policy consensus. Massive intervention to support the dollar by the European central banks led to accelerating money supply growth outside the United States, and ultimately to higher world inflation. Continually realigning currencies to adjust for mismatches in government policies was doomed to failure — agreement on broad policy issues is integral to any system of pegged exchange rates.

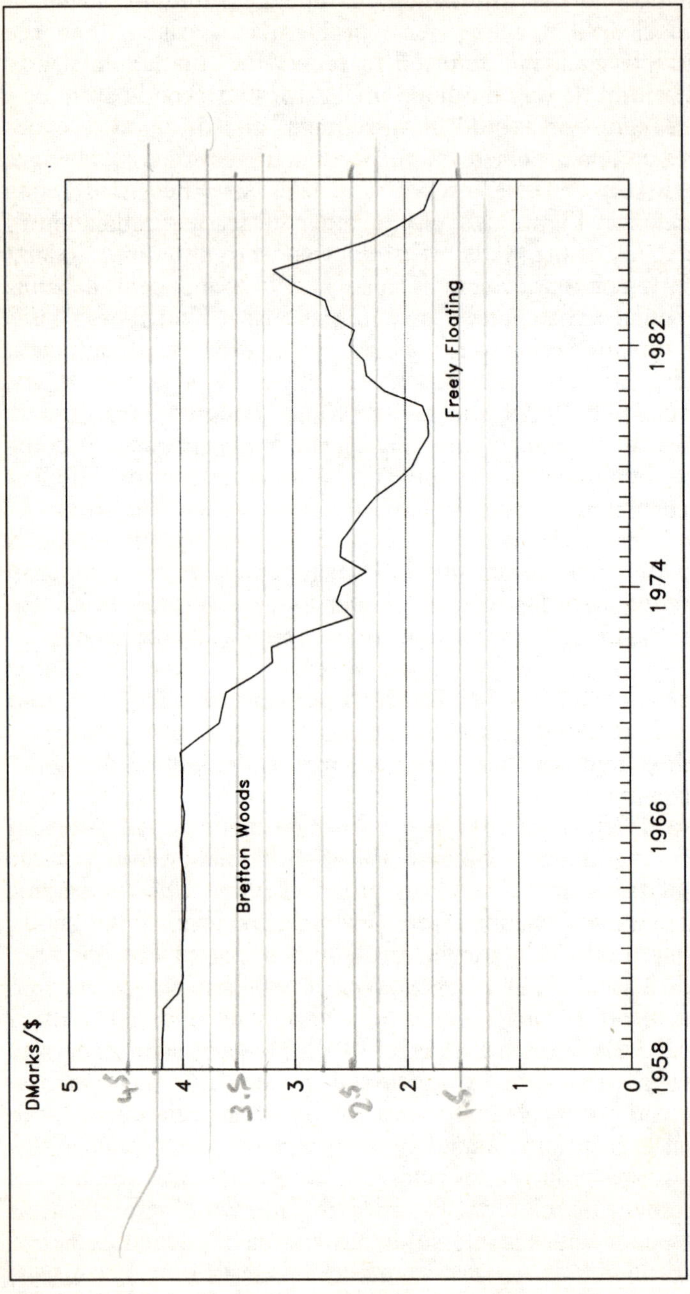

Figure 5.2 Thirty years of dollar/DMark rates 1958–1988

The European 'Snake'

Did the 'Snake' fail? It certainly has a rather chequered history and tends to be skimmed over in official histories of European monetary co-operation. It was born in rather difficult circumstances as the breakdown of Bretton Woods had unleashed unprecedented short-term volatility in the world currency markets. In the 1972 Basle Agreement, six countries (Belgium, France, Germany, Italy, Luxembourg and the Netherlands) agreed to contain the fluctuations of their bilateral rates within a $2\frac{1}{4}$ per cent band, the 'Snake', while their rates against the dollar moved within a $4\frac{1}{2}$ per cent band, the 'Tunnel'. Before long the dollar link was dropped and this became a European co-ordination system, with a European Monetary Co-operation Fund being established in 1973 to provide short-term finance to central banks. Membership for many countries proved short-lived. Italy departed in January 1973. France left the system in January 1974, rejoined in July 1975 and left again in March 1976. By 1978 only a 'mini-snake' remained and, in contrast to Bretton Woods, this was a hard-currency bloc, with the Deutschmark dominating the other minor currencies in the system. Realignments had become commonplace as the minor currencies tried to keep pace with the Deutschmark.

Clearly an important element in a successful pegged exchange rate system is credibility. Early departures from the system undermined market confidence and thus increased the cost (through higher interest rates) of membership to those remaining. Having broken the taboo of leaving the system, the political cost of future defections had been reduced. This 'defection' problem is one which the ERM had managed to avoid until mid-1992 and thus the recent ERM crisis has rather unhappy historical parallels. The discussion in this chapter has centred on the role of the exchange rate in helping economies adjust to external shocks. In the wake of the 1973 oil shock, there was just such a realignment within the 'Snake' as the Norwegian krone was revalued by 5 per cent. But the instability of the system largely centred on divergent policy choices, such as the trade-off between growth and inflation, rather than the impact of external shocks. Thus, the failure of the franc's participation can be traced back to the conflict between the demands of the Snake and the French government's concern to meet domestic economic objectives. It is clear that the outlook for the ERM is very much dependent on continuing pan-European policy co-operation.

One criticism of the Snake at the time was that the Deutsch-mark had come to dominate the system. While the Bundesbank did intervene to support weaker currencies, ultimately the burden of policy adjustment fell upon the smaller economies such as Denmark and Sweden. There were heavy inflows out of the dollar into the Deutschmark throughout this period so these were rather exceptional circumstances. However, it may well be that the 'asymmetry' of the Snake is a problem which was never fixed. If the dollar lent an inflationary bias to Bretton Woods, are German monetary policies leading to deflation throughout Europe?

SUMMARY: THE CASE FOR CURRENCY ADJUSTMENTS

- The exchange rate plays an important role in pro-moting economic adjustment and losing this will have a cost, creating volatility elsewhere and slowing the appropriate economic changes.
- There are similarities in European economies but country-specific shocks will still occur, indeed there has just been a major German shock in reunifica-tion. Preventing the exchange rate response has a high cost relative to the benefits of a stable currency outlined in Chapter 4.
- Substitutes for exchange rate changes, such as down-ward flexibility in wages, are unlikely to be effective in the short-term, although a pan-European fiscal policy may ease economic adjustments.
- Failures of pegged exchange rate regimes largely reflect divergent national policy choices, rather than differences in economic structure. This suggests that the future of European monetary union may hinge on the relationship between national and pan-European economic policy.

Chapter
SIX

NATIONAL ECONOMIC POLICY WITHIN THE ERM

●●●

POLICY CO-OPERATION IN THE NEW EUROPE

In a Europe with close economic ties between countries there
will inevitably be a need for policy co-operation. Any policy
change in one country will quickly impact on the economic
performance of another. The question is: what form will this
co-operation take? The leaders of the world's largest economies
meet regularly to discuss world economic developments, hoping
to tackle economic challenges as a group rather than individu-
ally. This co-ordination tends to be flexible, at its most informal
when simply exchanging views, but also capable of agreeing
immediate steps in the wake of a common crisis, such as the
1987 Stock Market crash. The European Community, in
contrast, has been set on a path of economic co-operation based
on rules, the most important of which is the commitment to
maintain stable exchange rates within the ERM. The difference
between these two approaches was thrown into sharp relief by
the events of December 1991.

In the autumn of that year, the Bundesbank had become
increasingly concerned at the level of wage settlements and the
pace of money supply growth in Germany. To a large degree
these developments reflected the impact of reunification, and
were not matched in the rest of Europe. The acceleration
in money supply growth, for example, was primarily due to
lending for investment in the former East Germany. In contrast,
growth outside Germany was proving disappointedly sluggish
with a real danger that the United States would slip back into

recession. Ahead of the Bundesbank meeting in the third week of December, there was mounting international pressure on the Germans not to raise interest rates. The aftermath of this meeting — the first since the Maastricht Treaty was agreed — demonstrated the extent to which the European central banks had lost the ability to set interest rates independently of Germany.

The Bundesbank judged that the fight against domestic inflation required a tightening of policy and increased its official short-term interest rates by $\frac{1}{2}$ per cent. The discount rate, the floor for German interest rates, was raised to 8 per cent, the highest level since the Great Depression. Immediately following the surprise announcement, the Netherlands, Denmark, Belgium and Austria all increased their rates by the same amount. The other EC governments hesitated, torn between their hope for lower interest rates to help domestic growth and their ERM commitments which pointed to higher rates. Within the week, France, Italy and Spain had been forced to tighten monetary policy to calm the currency markets. At an earlier international conference of economic leaders, the French and United States representatives had many of the same concerns about the outlook for world growth and hoped that lower interest rates would contribute to a recovery. While France was ultimately compelled to raise interest rates because of its desire to maintain a stable franc, the United States' central bank acted boldly, slashing its discount rate by a full percentage point to $3\frac{1}{2}\%$.

The Maastricht Treaty and full monetary union will further impinge on national economic policy, limiting autonomy amid raising fears that national economic sovereignty is at stake. In this chapter, we consider in turn how monetary and fiscal policy will be constrained and assess the framework for setting pan-European policy in a 'united' Europe.

MONETARY POLICY: THE ERM 'STRAIT-JACKET'

As the ERM evolves into a single currency, individual countries will:

- no longer be able to chose national inflation trends;
- be able to reduce inflation at a lower cost in unemployment;
- lose a means of managing short-term economic developments;
- and outside Germany, gain influence over the direction of European monetary policy.

We can no longer choose our long-term inflation rate

When the Bretton Woods system of fixed exchange rates broke down in 1973, countries were able to make their own choices about inflation again. As Figure 6.1 illustrates, in response to the oil shocks several European economies allowed inflation to rise dramatically.

Within a system of fixed exchange rates, differences in trend inflation rates will not be sustained. If prices rise more rapidly in Italy than in Germany, Italian exports become increasingly uncompetitive and Italy's trade position deteriorates. This deterioration puts downward pressure on the currency, and ultimately Italian economic policy will have to be tightened in order to defend the currency and bring down domestic inflation. According to Purchasing Power Parity, in the long run:

Italian Inflation = Rate of Lira Depreciation + German Inflation

and if the lira's external value is fixed, then the two inflation rates must be roughly equal.

This is clearly a loss of economic sovereignty — but does it matter? In general, economists agree that there is little value in being able to choose a higher long-term inflation rate than the rest of Europe. To begin with, they draw a distinction between nominal and real changes in the economy: Nominal variables are the general level of prices, money supply, the exchange rate, wages. Real variables include national output, unemployment, household purchases of washing machines.

In an economy with 8 per cent inflation, provided money supply, wages and prices are all growing at the same rate, there may be no difference in the way real variables (such as national

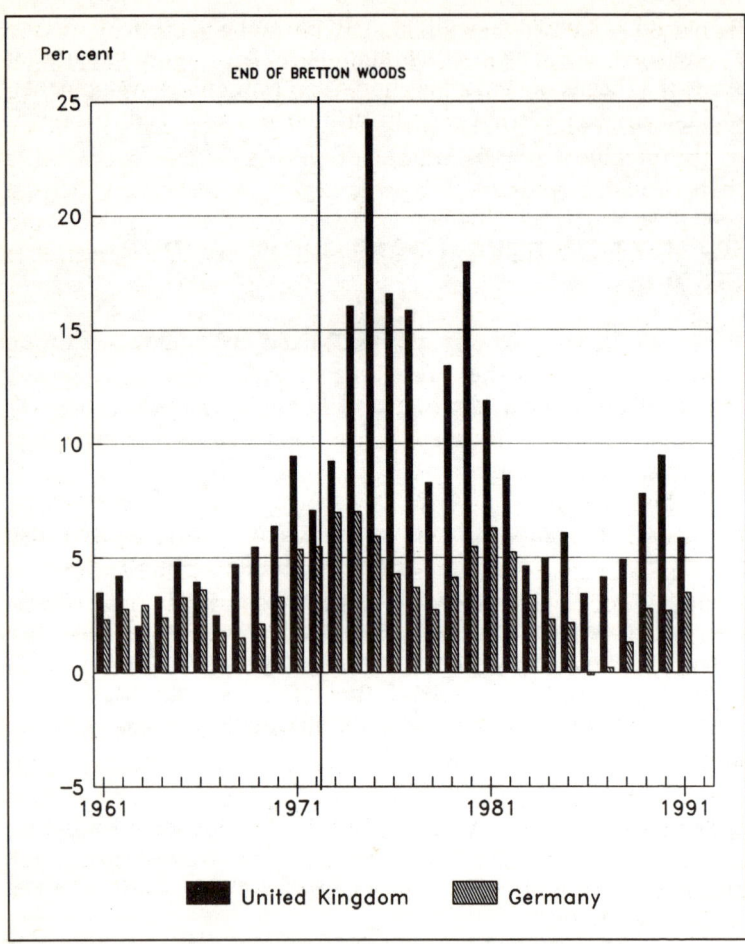

Figure 6.1   Inflation choices: UK and Germany

output) develop compared with a 4 per cent inflation economy. As a result, living standards in the two countries are the same.

However, as inflation starts to accelerate above 10 per cent, the cost of inflation becomes increasingly high. Shops have to change prices more often, banks have to cope with more cash withdrawals, and distortions creep into the way companies make business decisions. The greatest economic impact though comes with *unexpected* inflation — a sharp jump in prices which has not been anticipated. When this occurs firms faced with an increased price for their goods are unsure whether this is due to greater demand or higher inflation in the economy as a whole. Wealth is also redistributed as the value of certain types of financial asset fails to rise with prices. For pensioners the value of the income from government bonds is largely fixed, while their capital investment will be declining in real terms. Strong growth and high inflation sometimes go together — between the two oil crises, Japan grew at an average $3\frac{1}{2}$ per cent per annum with inflation touching 10 per cent. But this inflation may have been a hindrance to economic expansion.

It is sometimes argued that there are European countries, such as Germany, which are simply happier with a lower rate of inflation. Greece, Spain and Portugal, it is said, have higher inflation rates as a reflection of their particular economic structures and institutions. The truth of the matter, however, is that inflation has become 'institutionalized' as a result of past policy mistakes. Greece is a high inflation country with 20 per cent inflation in 1990, but in the 1960s prices there rose at a meagre 2 per cent annual rate. For these countries, only a long-term commitment to low inflation will wring out the inflationary biases. They may therefore have most to gain from the path to monetary union.

An individual European nation's freedom to choose a long-term inflation rate is compromised by the Maastricht agreement, but if the ERM guarantees stable low inflation then it may actually work to the nation's benefit. This is rather similar to giving up personal liberties, the freedom to take drugs for example, as a form of self-protection and to ensure a better society as a whole.

Transition to low inflation and credibility

Many of the higher inflation countries in the European Community have attempted to bring down the rate of inflation over the past decade. The authorities often face a problem of convincing everyone in the economy that the rate of price increases is going to be reduced — they must dampen inflationary expectations. If workers demand a 15 per cent pay increase, and companies finance this level of settlements by raising their prices in turn by 15 per cent then this quickly becomes established as the general rate of inflation. When the central bank announces that it will reduce inflation to 5 per cent, it faces a *credibility* problem. If national policy-makers lack credibility, then interest rates (and perhaps taxes) will have to be raised to demonstrate their determination to bear down on inflation. Companies trying to increase their prices by 15 per cent may find difficulty doing so as these policy measures weaken domestic demand and as a result may have to lay off workers. In this way, reducing nominal inflation starts to impact on real variables, creating unemployment and depressing national output. This is only a 'transitional cost', but will be paid until inflationary expectations are finally brought down.

ERM membership may help with the credibility problem. Once a currency has joined the mechanism, adjustments can only occur with the agreement of the other EC finance ministers. A realignment has a broader political cost as it comes with adverse publicity and a sense of crisis: in the wake of the 1983 franc devaluation President Mitterrand was described in the daily press as 'a rather isolated, ashen figure closeted in the Elysee and finding it difficult to maintain his moorings'. Accepting the ERM discipline thus makes it much more difficult for the central bank concerned to abandon its anti-inflationary policy. The participation of the lira in the ERM throughout the 1980s may well have helped the authorities' fight against inflation and is described in greater detail later in this chapter.

The political cost of an ERM realignment may have been high before the Maastricht Treaty, but the terms of monetary union have further raised this cost. A country wishing to play a full part in the steps to a single currency must have an inflation rate within $1\frac{1}{2}$ per cent of the average of the three lowest rates. Its currency should not have been devalued within the ERM over the previous two years. National policy-makers asking for a devaluation to compensate for higher inflation thus risk being left behind on the path to closer European integration. It is confidence in the Maastricht inflation targets and the political imperative that they must be achieved, which is currently bearing down on inflationary expectations throughout Europe.

Short-term economic management

There may well be a price to pay for the anchor of exchange rate stability. While governments may be able to reduce domestic inflation more quickly, their scope to deal with short-term fluctuations in economic conditions has been reduced. ERM critics argue that governments not only lose a means of influencing the domestic economy, but the way that the ERM operates over the short term creates severe policy dilemmas.

The loss of a policy tool

National governments have often made a whole series of promises to the electorate: lower inflation, stronger economic growth, low unemployment et al. To achieve these targets they only have a limited number of variables they can directly influence: taxes, public spending, interest rates and the foreign exchanges. Locking the currency into the ERM and setting interest rates to defend it, significantly reduces the number of policy instruments the government has to hand. The United Kingdom as an oil producer was hit by the sharp fall in oil prices in 1986, but the government cushioned this blow by allowing sterling to lose ground on the currency markets.

Gained a policy dilemma?

The short-term policy dilemmas hinge on the dynamics of the system. Alan Walters, the distinguished UK economist, argues that the problem with the ERM is that it is neither one thing nor the other. Currencies are neither allowed to float freely against each other, nor are they fixed permanently. As a result, interest rate differentials simply reflect market confidence in the system. If the market believes there is no risk of a realignment, then capital will flow into high yielding ERM currencies. Interest rates in high inflation economies, such as Spain, will be brought down to German levels, but this easing of Spanish monetary policy will undermine the fight against domestic inflation and ultimately prevent convergence between the two economies. The Walters critique suggests that, perversely, it is only the fear of realignments which allows countries such as Spain and Italy to keep relatively high interest rates.

There is a further short-term problem, which again hinges on the 'market confidence' issue. A weak economic performance in a particular EC country may begin to undermine popular support for its government policies, and indeed for the ERM commitment itself. As these pressures undermine confidence in the currency, the authorities have to demonstrate their determination to defend the existing parties by raising short-term interest rates. The economic slowdown will be intensfied by this monetary tightening, further weakening government support and undermining confidence in the ERM.

This discussion suggests that the ERM has advantages as a framework for long-term economic policy at the national level. However, its lack of flexibility in the short-term may lead to policy decisions which are clearly inappropriate from a domestic perspective.

Setting monetary policy in Europe

As the experience of the ERM members in December 1991 demonstrated, European monetary policy is being heavily influenced by the Bundesbank. In turn, the Bundesbank's primary obligation is to preserve the domestic value of the Deutschmark.

Pleas by Germany's neighbours to take into account sluggish European economic growth, not only failed to prevent this tightening but also a further $\frac{3}{4}$ per cent rise in the discount rate in mid-1992. In the wake of German reunification, it has become increasingly apparent that European interest rates are being set to contain German inflation and are not a reflection of pan-European inflationary pressures.

This outcome is rather surprising. The Bretton Woods system of fixed exchange rates had the dollar at its centre, and governments pegged their currencies against the dollar. But the European Monetary System and the ERM intervention grid is designed to be symmetrical. If the lira reaches its floor against the Deutschmark then both the Bank of Italy and the Bundesbank are obliged to intervene to support the lira and weaken the DMark. In practice, the Bundesbank's unwillingness to adopt a more accommodative monetary policy in the face of currency pressures has left the DMark as the key (or 'anchor') ERM currency. Policy-makers hoping to avoid an ERM realignment are thus forced to match German interest changes.

At the second stage of monetary union, the new European Monetary Institute is mandated to 'strengthen the co-ordination of monetary policies' and will provide a setting for the discussion of the economic outlook. When the Institute finally evolves into the European Central Bank, individual countries will lose all independence in monetary policy. However, ECU interest rates will be set by the Governing Council of the ECB (which includes the national central bank governors) and will now be based on inflation and growth prospects throughout the Community. German dominance will have finally given way to a true pan-European monetary policy.

CASE STUDY — THE ITALIAN EXPERIENCE

At the end of the 1970s, not only was a European Central Bank a distant ideal, Italian involvement appeared extremely unlikely. As Figures 6.2 and 6.3 indicate, there was a substantial differential between Italian and German inflation rates, and this was in turn reflected in substantially higher long-term lira interest rates. After ten years of ERM membership, Italian inflation has been trimmed to only $6\frac{1}{2}$ per cent, although its unemployment rate has risen along with that in the rest of Europe. The Italian experience demonstrates the advantages — and some of the limitations — of joining the Exchange Rate Mechanism in implementing national monetary policy.

The main source of Italy's difficulties in the 1970s lay with the failure of the Bank of Italy to set a rigorous anti-inflationary course. As a result, workers had looked to change the system of wage bargaining to protect their standards of living. The 'scala mobile' (or wage escalator) automatically increased the level of wages to reflect inflationary trends and had been operating since the 1950s. Following the second oil shock, the unions and employers agreed to revamp this system and by 1977 roughly nine-tenths of inflation was feeding through directly to domestic wage increases. Not only did the lira not participate in the European Snake arrangement, but the Italian wage-price spiral led to periodic lira crises.

Given this history, it was not too surprising that the decision to join the ERM *by itself* did little to help the Italian authorities' credibility. In the wake of the 1979 oil crisis, inflation accelerated sharply again, averaging just over 20 per cent in 1980. The wider band for the lira (at ± 6 per cent) and successive realignments undermined the ERM commitment as a guide for future inflationary trends. However, the Bank of Italy did ensure that the extent of the lira devaluations failed to fully allow for

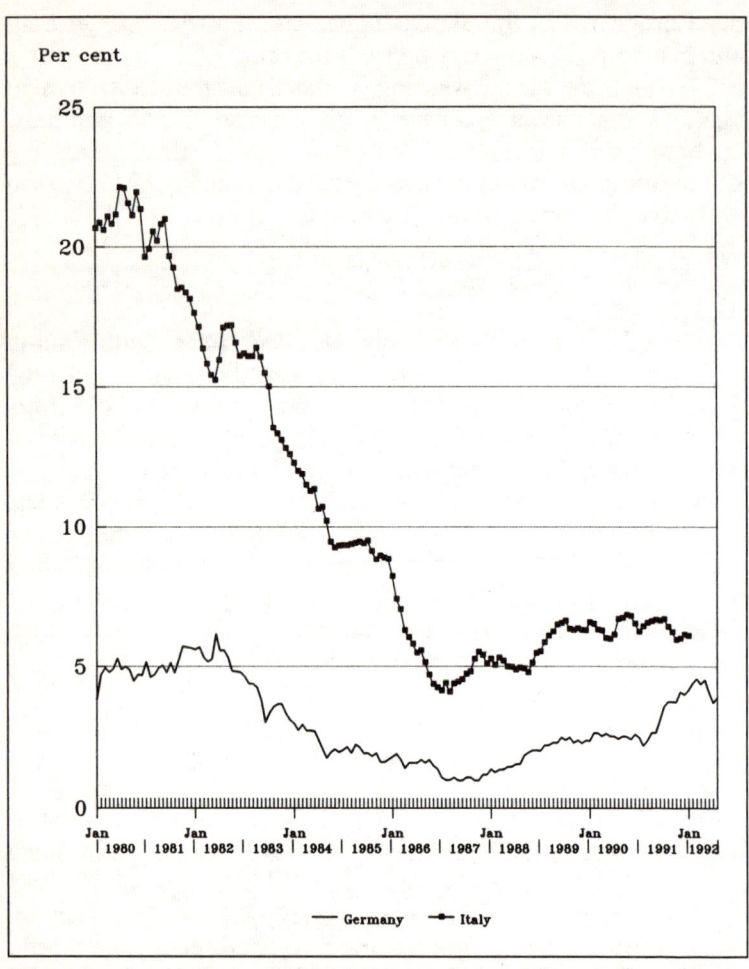

Figure 6.2 Relative inflation performance: Italy and Germany

the pace of domestic wage increases. As a result, Italian companies selling in export markets had to raise their prices in foreign currency terms and faced the prospect of losing market share.

The breakthrough for the Italian authorities came in the years 1983 to 1986, when the 'scala mobile' was heavily modified. The desire to see economic convergence in Europe played a role in these modifications — wage indexation was related to official inflation targets which in turn were based on a planned

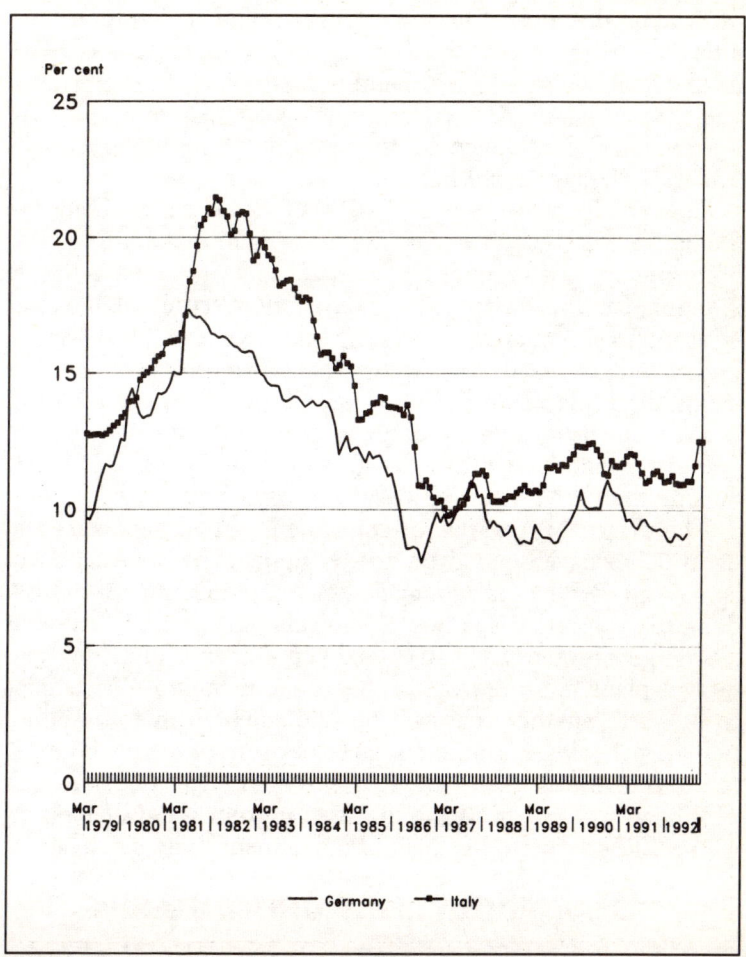

Figure 6.3   Long yields — Italy and Germany

narrowing of the Italian-EC inflation gap. The government's tough approach, reinforced by a favourable national referendum in mid-1985, led to further radical changes for the scala mobile in the public sector. These reforms, along with global disinflationary trends, brought Italian inflation down to below 5 per cent in 1987.

The Italian government's anti-inflation credibility was reflected not only in lower price rises, but also in lira interest rates. The differential between German and Italian long-term interest rates narrowed significantly, to just 3 per cent in 1990. In that year the lira's ERM band was narrowed to $2\frac{1}{4}$ per cent, and the remaining restrictions on capital flows were removed. International confidence in the economy's performance was evident in heavy capital inflows.

Could this convergence have been achieved without the Exchange Rate Mechanism? The answer must be yes, as any independent government or central bank is free to tackle inflation. But the exchange rate commitment represented a clear indication of a change in policy regime. The ERM gave the Italian authorities the right external environment for undertaking domestic institutional change. There has been a cost of bearing down on inflation, both in term of unemployment and periods of subdued economic growth, but the costs for Italy outside the ERM may well have been significantly higher.

The external pressures for adjustment of both monetary and fiscal policy have been given greater impetus by the Maastricht agreement and the lira's dramatic exit from the ERM re-inforced domestic calls for a solution to the economic 'crisis'. The new Amato government has had considerable success in getting new budget plans approved by the Italian parliament — it remains to be seen whether they will be implemented in full. With a public borrowing requirement at 11 per cent of national output, the next major challenge for Italy will be to meet EC standards in this area of policy. If the lira is to make a *sustainable* return to the ERM, a period of painful adjustment must lie ahead.

FISCAL POLICY IN A UNITED EUROPE

The monetary union and budget policy linkages

When recession hits an EC economy, it is unlikely that the unemployed will demonstrate outside the buildings of the new European Central Bank. Not least because the local social security payments won't cover the plane fare to the ECB. Instead, they are likely to turn to their national Parliaments for action. With governments now only responsible for fiscal policy — government taxes and expenditure — there is a danger that they boost spending and increase public borrowing to help the domestic economy. As a result, while ECU interest rates are likely to be stable and standard throughout the Community, government deficits could be more volatile and, perhaps, eventually prove too large to be sustainable.

There is a further link between monetary union and the state of national public finances. If a government has a very large outstanding public debt and is unable to bring revenues and spending into line, it may benefit from higher inflation in the economy. An unexpected jump in inflation reduces the 'real' value of government debt; when investors in public debt are finally repaid they will be able to buy less than they had expected because of the higher prices. As a result, very large public debts may lead to pressure on the central banks to 'bail-out' national governments. When in a unified Europe all debt is ECU debt, there could well be pressure on the ECB to soften its anti-inflation policies.

The Maastricht Treaty recognises the link between monetary union and national fiscal policy. As outlined in Chapter 2, the Treaty's criteria for assessing economic convergence include information on public finances. Government deficits should represent less than 3 per cent of national output and total outstanding debt should be less than 60 per cent of national output. But when the conditions for monetary union are met — what happens then? Just as Maastricht has a strong anti-inflation stance, it takes a strong line on fiscal policy: 'Member States shall avoid excessive government deficits'.

National fiscal policy after EMU

The European policeman for fiscal policy is to be the European Council of Ministers (which includes representatives from each country). The Council will review the balance between government taxes and spending in each country and, if necessary, declare that an excessive deficit exists. The Council is planned to be part social worker and part policeman. Initially, it recommends action to correct the problem, but if insufficient action is taken it 'imposes fines of an appropriate size'. Whether these fines will further add to the public debt remains an open question.

National policy-makers retain control of budgetary policy, though under the benevolent gaze of the European institutions. The introduction of a single currency may actually make fiscal policy much more flexible in the short term. When national currencies are abandoned, all government debt will be issued in the ECU bond markets and will be financed at long-term ECU interest rates. Capital will flood in from across Europe to fund the temporary government debt. This is in contrast to the current situation, where heavy government borrowing can quickly put upward pressure on national long-term interest rates. Foreign investors are hesitant to fund the deficit as they must buy the local currency — and run the risk of a devaluation. Note that cheaper short-term funding is only available because the debt is denominated in ECUs. The option of solving long-term debt problems through inflation is thus no longer open — the European Central Bank is putting a lid on ECU inflation. The impact of a monetary union will be very different for individual EC countries, as there is an additional link between inflation and the budget deficit. Commercial banks in each country are compelled to hold non-interest bearing accounts at their national central bank. When prices rise the real value of these accounts, along with holdings of notes and coins, is reduced. As a result of inflation, spending power is being redistributed from the private sector to the central bank, and ultimately helps finance the government deficit. This is sometimes referred to an 'inflation tax' and the higher the inflation the greater the tax revenues. When countries such as Greece join the monetary union, they will have to substantially increase income and VAT taxes, thus adjusting their public finances to the new low inflation regime.

Economists have tried to guess what problems will be created by leaving national governments free to set their own budgets. The main thrust of the Maastricht Treaty is to prevent excessive profligacy, perhaps reflecting the experience of the last two decades. However, experts in the public policy field are also concerned that government spending may be cut down too far in the unified Europe. People and companies are now free to do business anywhere in the EC, and naturally they will favour the low tax countries. As governments 'compete' to attract businesses, they may well cut back on education and training to lower direct taxes. This suggests that Europe may have to set agreed minimum levels of taxes and public services in each country, as well as helping to solve 'excessive deficits'.

The pan-European fiscal policy

The extent to which there will be a new European budget, raising its own taxes and spending throughout the Community, has yet to be determined. Central EC spending currently represents only 1 per cent of total output, and recent attempts to expand this budget significantly have failed. This is rather disconcerting as a pan-European budget could help individual countries adjust to local economic shocks, instead of devaluing. Successful major monetary unions such as the United States tend to have a federal safety net in place. It has been estimated that when a US region's income falls by a dollar, as much as 40 cents of this decline is offset by the Federal government. Access to the new ECU bond market may give national governments flexibility in responding to shocks, but in the early years of the new single currency area it may become apparent that a pan-European 'insurance policy' is required.

NATIONAL SOVEREIGNTY AND FEDERALISM

Currency and national sovereignty

In the new unified Europe, there will be some role for national fiscal policy, but, in the final stage of monetary union, national currencies will be replaced by the ECU. Abolishing the pound sterling or the Deutsch-mark raises much broader issues than the direct economic impact of permanently fixing exchange rates. Enoch Powell, the British MP, argued in the House of Commons that:

> There is nothing which comes nearer to sovereignty, self-government, or what politics is about than control of money. From the beginning of times it has been the attribute of sovereigns that they made or declared money ... there is nothing more directly and clearly inimical to the political process in this country than the professed intention to enter into a monetary union.

This might be dismissed as an example of British insularity, but the same theme was heard in the months following the Maastricht agreement. In an attempt to reassure Germans afraid of losing the stable Deutschmark, the German Finance Minister, Theo Waigel, argued that those countries participating in monetary union would have to meet very strict criteria:

> Only those who are recognised as being 'qualified for Europe' after a strict and incorruptible examination, before 1999, will get the new Euromark from the European central bank, set up according to our own design.

Despite these reassurances, opinion polls in Germany indicate that a large majority favour retaining the Deutschmark.

In planning the pace of monetary union, this caution must be taken into consideration. While fixing exchange rates always leaves the option of withdrawal from the system, losing control of the national currency represents a far more fundamental development. The suggestion that ECUs will carry the imprint of the issuing central bank fails to disguise the importance of this step.

A premature move to a single currency may undermine the major benefits which monetary union is designed to bring (see Chapter 4). According to the ECU-enthusiasts, in the Europe of the early 21st century, businesses in the Community will no longer have to worry about a surge in Itialian inflation or an acceleration in French credit growth. The policy backdrop throughout Europe will be relatively stable. Companies will now be able to plan ahead with greater confidence as they subsequently increase their investment programmes, European output will be higher as a result. But sweeping away national autonomy will only yield policy stability if the new federal policy-making institutions work well.

The United States has considerable experience of setting monetary policy at the federal level and indeed there are similarities between the planned ECB and its central bank, the Federal Reserve Board. There are 12 regional 'central banks' in the US, but official dollar interest rates are set centrally by a committee in Washington. The committee includes five regional representatives (chosen in rotation), along with the Federal Reserve Governors chosen by the President. The regional banks regularly report on local business conditions, recommend changes in the discount rate and attempt to influence federal policy through publishing research. In a similar way, national economic concerns in individual European countries will be fed through to the ECB.

What happens when there are strong differences of opinion between regions? In the early years of the US system, the regional 'central banks' had considerable autonomy and could even lend on their own terms. The central committee's role was relatively restricted and the power to determine monetary policy became very fragmented. This decentralization proved a disaster and the resulting policy paralysis may have contributed to the severity of the Great Depression. Reforms reinforcing the power of the Washington-based policy committee succeeded in restoring the stability of the system.

The US experience suggests that when a single currency is introduced, national concerns may influence ECU interest rates but ultimately the hard decisions will be taken at the centre — at the European Central Bank. The abandonment of national currencies will require not only economic convergence, but a broad-based political confidence in the new European institutions.

CONCLUSION

- The high degree of economic integration within Europe makes international co-operation essential — further steps to currency union will heavily limit freedom to alter national economic policies, particularly monetary policy.
- Those countries following the Maastricht route will no longer be able to choose their long-term inflation performances, but anti-inflationary policies will have greater credibility.
- A more important loss is in control over interest rates in the short term, particularly as within the Exchange Rate Mechanism a country's influence

over interest rate developments in the rest of
Europe may be relatively weak.

- The Italian experience in the 1980s illustrates how
the ERM discipline creates a suitable external
environment in which domestic institutional change
can occur.

- National public spending and taxes will ultimately
be used more actively in managing individual economies. In response to short-term economic fluctuations, national fiscal policy may actually be more
flexible, though there will be pan-European rules
to prevent unsustainable public sector deficits
developing.

- Following monetary union the economic policy
trade-offs will be dominated by decisions made
at the centre — abandoning national currencies
requires broad-based political confidence in the
new EC institutions.

Part
THREE

··

THE BROADER INTERNATIONAL CONTEXT FOR THE ERM

··

Chapter
SEVEN

REGIONAL DISPARITIES AND MONETARY UNION

●●

THE BROADER ISSUES FOR MONETARY UNION

The Maastricht Treaty suggests that the Exchange Rate Mechanism is a vital building-block for European monetary union. If this is indeed the case, then each country cannot just make a narrow economic calculation about the ERM based on saved transaction costs or reduced policy autonomy; much broader issues are at stake. In this and the next two chapters, we look at the following areas:

- the role of the existing less-prosperous regions in the new monetary union;
- the new applications for Community membership from EFTA, eastern and southern Europe;
- the ECU in a world of regional trading blocs.

Without considering these issues, what may be to the temporary advantage of a single nation within the Community could eventually prove to have a much higher long-term cost. Equally, international policy developments during the inter-war years arguably laid the conditions for profound economic and political instability. Setting aside your preconceptions about the current structure of the Community consider the economic data for a selection of European countries laid out in Table 7.1. On the assumption that France and Germany are at the heart of the monetary union, which countries would you consider adding next?

Most readers will have probably placed Austria and Sweden at the head of the list, with Hungary nudging Greece out of last

Table 7.1 Economic indicators for seven European countries

	Standard of living (US = 100)	Inflation (%)	Exports (% GDP)	Agricultural employment (% total)
France	72	3.2	22.6	6.4
West Germany	75	4.8	35.5	3.7
Austria	68	4.1	46.1	8.0
Greece	35	18.3	21.7	25.3
Hungary	30	35	15.0	18.0
Portugal	37	8.5	36.5	19.0
Sweden	75	2.4	30.0	3.6

Source: OECD Country Reports

place. The timetable of the Maastricht Treaty suggests that the criteria for membership simply relate to economic management — inflation and government debt must have been brought down to levels which are consistent with stable exchange rates. But is this by itself sufficient? The table illustrates that these current economic indicators are only one aspect of the economy. The standard of living in Portugal and Greece is only half that in northern Europe, while there is a much heavier emphasis on agricultural employment, reflecting a lesser economic development. If wide differences in living standards are a potential problem for a single currency area, then perhaps these countries should be on the 'slow-lane' to monetary union. Even if this means being overtaken by Austria and Sweden.

The problem of choosing suitable countries for a currency union is not a new one. Experts in this field have long argued over the criteria which should be used in selecting the 'optimum currency area' — the group of countries for which the advantages of having a single currency outweigh the potential disadvantages. All new members should have:

1. a high level of trade, or financial flows, with existing countries;
2. open borders to inflows and outflows of workers with existing members;
3. an industrial structure which is not too specialised, or dissimilar to that elsewhere in the area;
4. similar policy views on the trade-off between inflation and unemployment.

Looking at the less prosperous countries in Europe, such as Portugal and Greece, on these criteria there are grounds for optimism. Once the commitments to the 1992 single market have been fulfilled, the first two conditions — of free trade and labour mobility — are likely to be met. There is a bias towards labour intensive manufacturing in these countries, but on the whole their industrial structures are not over-specialised in a single product area. When the Maastricht conditions are met, the less prosperous economies should play a full part in European monetary union.

However, the regional problem within Europe occurs at two levels. At the national level, Ireland, Spain, Greece and Portugal each have a standard of living less than 80 per cent of the EC average. However, there are also individual regions which have failed to match the post-war income gains in the rest of Europe — an important example is the Mezzogiorno region of southern Italy which has been receiving EC aid since the 1960s. An assessment of the economic patterns of Europe concluded that in 1983 the 'economic periphery' of the Community covered 40 per cent of its area, but represented only one-eighth of total output by value.

It is important for the ultimate success of an integrated Europe that these regional imbalances are *not* intensified by the transition to monetary union. The southern economies face particular challenges: transforming their domestic institutions and markets to accord with the new Europe, removing external barriers and, finally, meeting Maastricht policy targets. Fortunately, the experience of Portugal (described in detail later in this chapter) has given grounds for optimism.

THE STEPS TO MONETARY UNION

Market liberalisation

For Spain, Portugal and Greece there have been important steps in liberalising domestic competition over recent years. By tradition, their governments have played an important role in limiting the role of the free markets in allocating resources. In Greece, for example, the Ministry of Commerce had extensive influence, setting prices, determining profit margins, granting licences and quotas, and establishing powerful marketing boards for specific products. In order to comply with EC directives, the pace of deregulation has accelerated in each of these economies since mid-1985. The OECD estimates that 10 per cent of Greek household spending has been freed from price controls over the last two years. However, market prices have not always spurred competition, as the markets are often dominated by a few important producers or an industry association keen to agree on a new pricing structure. Spain may well point the way forward. It established a new Competition Law in 1989, which allows anyone to initiate procedures against anti-competitive practices, and can institute heavy fines. The financial services sector tends to be particularly inefficient in these economies, and the Spanish announcement that it will deregulate its insurance market is particularly welcome. Portugal has also embarked on an ambitious privatisation programme, across a broad spectrum of industries.

The transformation of market efficiency in these economies is likely to produce, over time, major improvements in living standards. International pressure — particularly EC directives — are providing the external environment for welcome domestic change.

The single European market

A greater challenge for producers lies in the removal of external barriers to competition. How the peripheral regions, including long-established members of the EC such as Ireland, fare in the single market is highly uncertain. There are a wide range of views ranging from the very gloomy to the very optimistic. At one extreme is the most pessimistic view. Manufacturers prefer to produce in large economic factories close to their major markets (and other manufacturers). With trade barriers removed and pan-European transport improved, they will produce in Germany for the local market exporting to Spain if there is demand. Any workers they need, they will attract into Germany from the peripheral regions, reinforcing the drift to the centre.

The more optimistic view argues that there are products in which the less-prosperous regions have a competitive advantage eg, labour intensive products. They will now be able to produce for the whole pan-European market not just the local market which will work to their advantage. Industries in the rest of Europe requiring cheap labour and land will relocate to Ireland or Spain.

Both arguments have some validity, which suggests that the impact of the single market will have to be monitored closely. EC funds currently supporting economic development in the less prosperous regions (outlined in the next section) may have to play an increased role in overcoming adjustment problems. Any negative repercussions of 1992 on living standards in the poorer regions, would represent an unwelcome widening of income differences within the European Community.

Monetary union

Lumping together these regions is rather inappropriate when it comes to monetary union. Ireland has made substantial progress towards meeting the Maastricht criteria, with inflation running at only $3\frac{1}{2}$ per cent. In this respect, it has more in common with the Netherlands than Greece. Nor are the arguments for and against monetary union in principle substantially different for the less prosperous regions. However, it can be argued that these arguments carry particular weight for these economies:

- The loss of government revenues from the 'inflation tax' (explained in Chapter 5) will be a powerful blow to public finances — as much as $1\frac{1}{4}$ per cent of national output in the case of Greece. This tax can be replaced by other forms of direct taxation (such as income tax), but these may prove less fair or more cumbersome to collect.
- The gains from macroeconomic stability in a single currency area may be very pronounced for the less prosperous regions. Accepting the discipline of the ERM may already have promoted international confidence in Spain and Portugal as it signalled a clear change in regime.
- In a period of considerable uncertainty, it may be wise for the southern economies to retain the option of a currency adjustment. The two-fold transition of internal market liberalisation and removal of external trade barriers will inevitably alter their international competitiveness. A later entry into monetary union would also allow policy-makers to draw on the experience of a more restricted single currency area.

There is already considerable experience of regional performance within monetary unions — most nations have depressed areas and their problems may appear intractable. For the lagging European regions, market and trade liberalisation carries with it the promise of improved living standards. However, within a broad monetary union *some* form of pan-European regional policy is likely to prove necessary. A 1973 EC meeting concluded that there would not be 'economic and monetary union without an adequate and effective regional policy backed by a fund with substantial resources'. If this is the case — how big will be the bill?

EC REGIONAL POLICY — WITH THE EMPHASIS ON COST!

The challenge for the European regional policy, as for national policy, is to invest for future growth in the depressed regions, rather than simply making transfers to support local income. The lagging regions have slipped into self-reinforcing cycles over the years. A disappointing economic performance has been reflected in reduced investment both in infrastructure (such as transport links) and education/training. The EC response has been to attempt to break this cycle with direct investment support. In 1975, the EC created the European Regional Development Fund (ERDF) with a remit to provide subsidies to stimulate investment and develop infrastructure in the less prosperous areas. Following the expansion of the Community to include Spain and Portugal, it was clear that regional policies would play a more important role in EC affairs and a major increase in spending was approved. There are also broader objectives for the Community, such as reducing long-term unemployment, which form part of its overall 'Structural Policy' and which particularly benefit the poorer regions. Thus the European Social Fund, set up primarily to tackle unemployment problems, will contribute to regional programmes.

By the standards of pan-European output the cost of these EC programmes is relatively small — although the EC budget doubled between 1988 and 1993 in real terms, it still only represents a small fraction of total EC output, 1.2 per cent. There has been a controversial debate as to whether this is sufficient given the magnitude of the income disparities within Europe. The MacDougall Report published in the mid-1970s argued that governments in single currency areas play a much more active role in ironing out income differentials. In long-established federations, national policies are reducing these disparities by as much as 35 per cent, a target out of reach of EC institutions given the size of their budget. Perhaps Europe should be following the example of the former West Germany, which in its drive to rapidly integrate the new east German länder is devoting $6\frac{1}{2}$ per cent of its national output.

What does Maastricht have to say? The Treaty restated the Community's commitment to 'reducing the disparities between the levels of development of the various regions'. As there is always room for another European Fund it also set up a Cohesion Fund to 'provide a financial contribution to projects in the fields of environment and trans-European networks in the area of transport infrastructure'. The Treaty itself does not call for a major increase in regional policy funding but in its wake, the Delors II finance package was proposed by the European Commission. This argued for another major increase in the overall EC budget lasting until 1997. While the total EC budget would rise by a third in real terms over this period, finance for structural and cohesion spending in the poorer regions would jump by more than half from ECU, 18.6bn to ECU 29bn at today's prices. At the Edinburgh summit this rise in spending was agreed but by 1999, and with the total EC budget limited to 1.271 of total output.

The recipients of these transfers are not in a political position to demand further sharp increases in EC investment. The major contributors to the EC budget, particularly Germany, face intense domestic pressures for public funds which is likely to prevail. But there is a further issue of efficiency. Increased capital inflows into less prosperous regions may serve to postpone important national policy adjustments. In the opinion of the OECD, 'EC transfers and loans have averted a balance-of-payments crisis in Greece', indeed two-thirds of its deficit on traded goods and services is being met by EC transfers. But these payments are slowing the pace of necessary policy adjustments. There is also a danger that a very rapid expansion of regional aid leads to less discrimination as to the type of

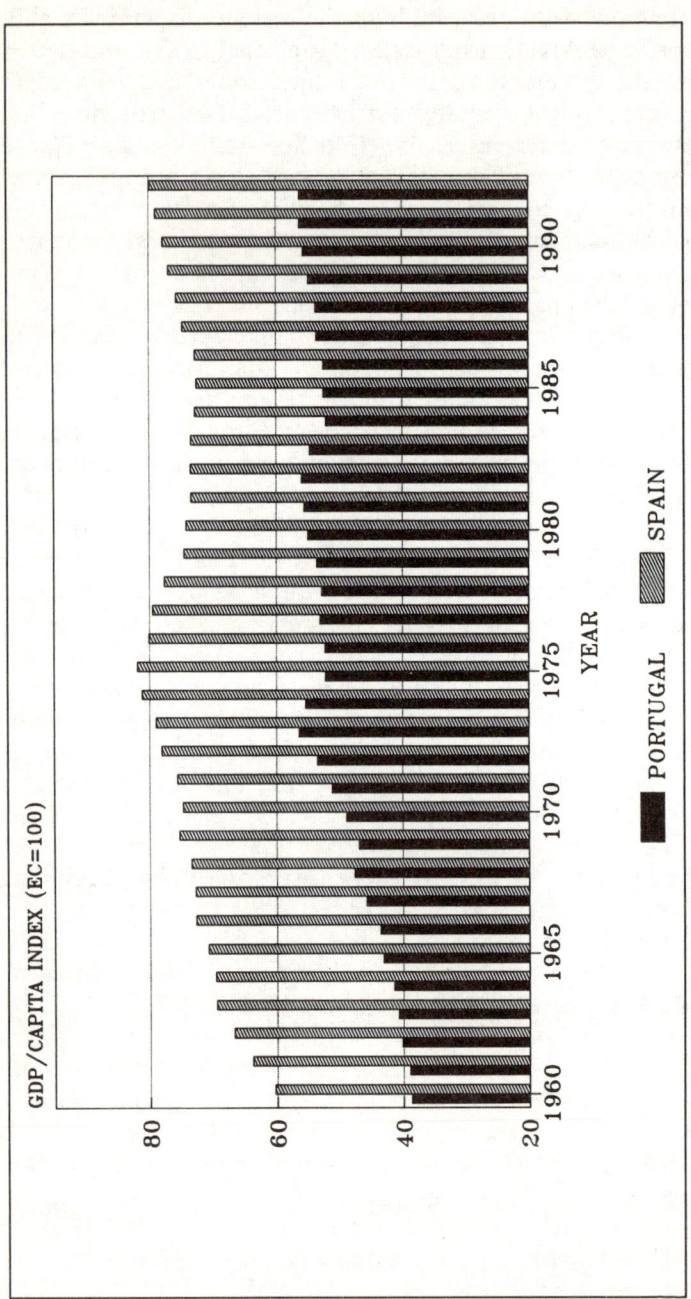

Figure 7.1 Gross Domestic Product per capita: Spain and Portugal

projects taken on. The EC has attempted to contain this problem by insisting that national governments also contribute to new projects, and that EC funding should not simply be used to free government spending for other uses. A recent report by the EC financial watchdog, the Court of Auditors, highlighted the fact that current regional subsidies could be used more efficiently.

Regional disparities may narrow to some degree as a result of EC policies, but more powerful influences are at work. Figure 7.1 outlines the development of living standards in Spain and Portugal since the 1960s, relative to the Community average. It appears that sustained pan-European growth during the 1960s reduced income disparities, with the turmoil following the two oil crises stalling the convergence. Making the right policy choices on the ERM and monetary union for the prosperous economies, will thus be very important for the peripheral European regions, as they may share disproportionately in the costs of failure.

CASE STUDY — PORTUGAL

The first oil shock not only brought economic turbulence to Portugal, but political turmoil. When power was seized by left-wing militants, there was widespread nationalisation while state intervention throughout the economy was greatly extended. Within two years a parliamentary democracy had been established, but the process of reversing these reforms proved relatively slow. As a result, when Portugal joined the European Community in 1986 it not only had a substantially lower standard of living but free markets played a much smaller role in determining the pattern of production. The past five years have thus brought dramatic changes in Portugal. Many aspects of the transition have been healthy, and give grounds for optimism that economic and monetary union will help the lagging regions.

We will look at three aspects of the recent changes:

1. the EC contribution to development;
2. government approach to policy adjustment;
3. investment and growth.

How the EC has helped

The European Community structural funds have played an important role in Portugal's economic development since 1986. The funds have been applied across a broad range of areas, not only tackling the public sector problems of infrastructure and education, but also promoting private sector modernisation and R&D spending. Over the past five years, structural fund payments have doubled to 2 per cent of GNP and are set to rise further under the terms of a special Community Support Framework. The significance of these inflows can be judged by comparison with Portuguese public spending. Of 14 billion ECUs spent on public works between 1989 and 1993, 7.4 billion ECUs will come directly from the EC. In addition, assistance has also been provided to help Portugal integrate its producers into the pan-European framework, a particular problem for the agricultural sector.

The government policy adjustment

This Portuguese government has been faced with a policy challenge in two areas: management of the economy and liberalisation of markets. Inflation in 1986 was still running at around 20 per cent, well above the EC average, but an anti-inflationary policy, along with favourable external factors, produced a sharp fall over subsequent years. Reflecting this success and in an attempt to maintain the Bank of Portugal's anti-inflation credibility, the escudo joined the Exchange Rate Mechanism in April 1992 and an escudo devaluation in November 1992 only occurred because of strong pressure from Spain to devalue both the escudo and peseta. Fiscal policy has remained rather lax by EC standards but funding has been provided in recent years by the new privatisation programme. Shifting companies from the public to the private sector has been underway since April 1989 and has touched many sectors, ranging from brewing to banking.

The results in growth and investment

It is clear that much has been done both by the EC and by the national authorities to tackle Portugal's inherited structural

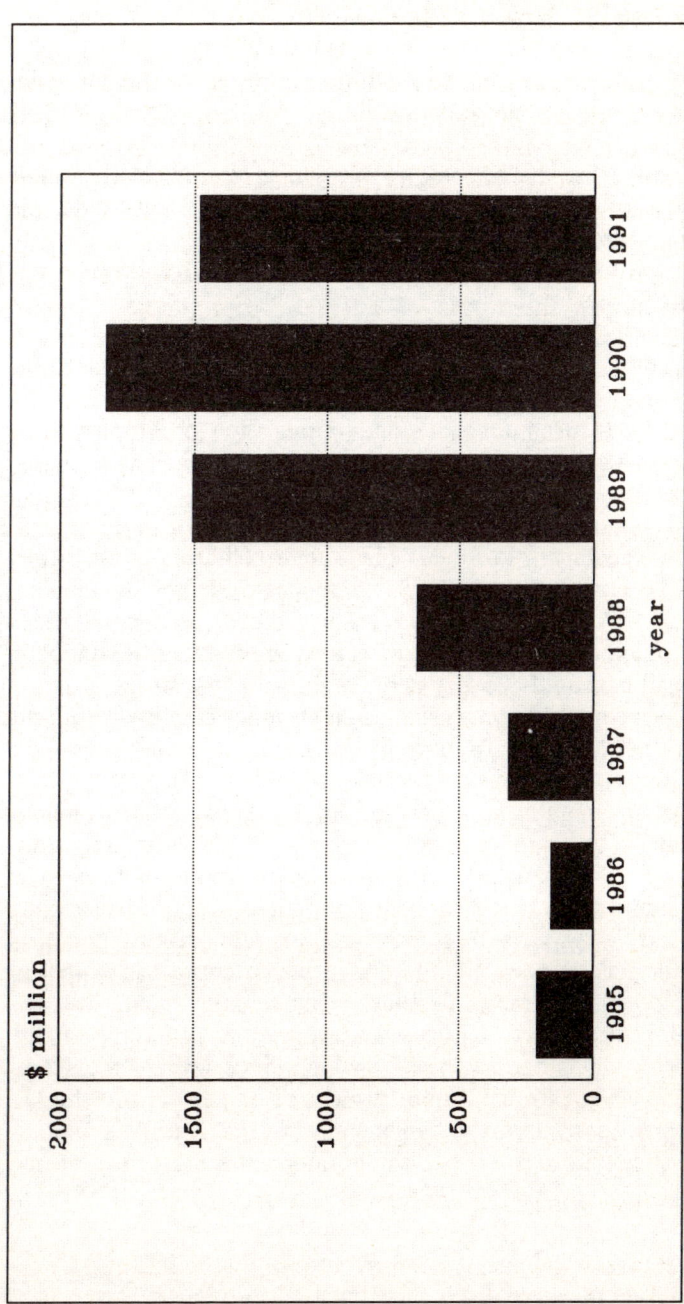

Figure 7.2 Foreign direct investment in Portugal 1985–1991

problems. But how will Portugal fare in the new integrated Europe, not only with a single market but also a single currency?

A key issue in the debate about the less prosperous economies has been whether producers will

1. move from the outlying regions to the centre of the single market (say Germany) to produce in larger plants and avoid transport costs; or
2. move to the peripheral regions to benefit from lower wage costs.

Portugal is a very low wage economy — at current exchange rates, private sector wages in Portugal are a quarter of those in Germany. It turns out that since joining the Community, there has been a surge in foreign investment in Portugal, as shown in Figure 7.2.

This is direct investment: companies buying or building production capacity in Portugal. This suggests that the wage differential is more than enough to compensate for any deficiencies in infrastructure or transport costs. Indeed, recent American data indicates that the rate of return from US investment in Portugal is roughly 25 per cent, against a pan-European figure of 20 per cent. The promise of greater policy stability within the EC framework may also have played a role in promoting inward investment.

Market liberalisation has led to efficiency improvements, notably in the banking sector, which should ultimately contribute to higher living standards. An expansion of trade with the Community has also been evident as trade barriers are removed — exports to Spain have proved buoyant and now account for 14 per cent of total exports, compared with just 4 per cent in 1985. While there must remain doubts over the longer-term impact of European integration, economic growth in Portugal has been relatively robust since joining the Community. With national output growth of $3\frac{3}{4}$ per cent in the last five years, there are grounds for optimism that Europe's regional disparities will narrow, not widen, along the road to monetary union.

SUMMARY: MONETARY UNION AND THE POOR REGIONS

- There are wide disparities in living standards and degrees of economic development within the Community. However, none of the economists' models of monetary unions suggest that this is necessarily a problem.
- The southern economies may benefit from market liberalisation, and the policy stability which the ERM framework demands. The implications of a single market are ambiguous, and there is a risk that more active European regional policies will be required.
- Plans for a substantial increase in spending on the less prosperous regions have been agreed although plans to increase the EC budget have been scaled back.
- The experience of Portugal gives grounds for optimism that the road to monetary union will bring a narrowing, not a widening, of regional disparities across Europe.

Chapter
EIGHT

THE IMPACT OF RENEWED EC EXPANSION

● ●

A COMMUNITY OF 30 MEMBER STATES?

The early months of 1985 brought two new Presidents to the centre of the European political stage. In the West, Jacques Delors took office as the new President of the European Commission. In the East, Gorbachev became President of the Soviet Union following the death of Chernenko. The Delors appointment gave additional impetus to EC integration. The following year the Community expanded to include Spain and Portugal and the signing of the Single Europe Act paved the way to an EC without national frontiers. In contrast, Gorbachev presided over the rapid disintegration of the Eastern trading bloc, known as COMECON, and then, in 1991, of the Soviet Union itself. These divergent fortunes left the Community facing a major external challenge in addition to the internal challenge of greater economic and monetary union. In the final months of 1991 the Community was not only negotiating the terms of the Maastricht Treaty but also involved in discussions formally and informally with potential new members in the West (the European Free Trade Area), in the former Eastern bloc (Hungary, Poland and Czechoslovakia) and within the Soviet Union itself (the Baltic States).

From the beginning it has been clear that the issues involved in redrawing the European map and the outlook for a single European currency have been extricably intertwined. On one level, the impact of these developments has been immediate and practical. While the terms for admitting the 16 million former East Germans was primarily discussed within a purely German (rather than a Community) setting, the terms on which the expansion occurred had widespread implications for the rest of Europe. The one-for-one exchange of East German 'Ostmarks' for Deutschmarks and the associated policy changes ultimately proved destabilising for the European Monetary System. While Europe had lost one currency in the Ostmark, the emerging nation states in the East created new currencies as an expression of national identity. Estonia, with a population of just $1\frac{1}{2}$ million, introduced the Estonian crown. The importance of a stable monetary framework for international trade was demonstrated acutely by a sharp contraction in trade between the Eastern block economies. The days of COMECON trade using the 'transferable rouble' were gone, but no replacement was immediately forthcoming.

The impact of east European developments on the monetary union debate has been much broader, however. The Community is now faced with applications from countries displaying an even greater diversity of economic development than existing members. External Affairs Commissioner, Frans Andriesson, argues that 'Europe is too heterogeneous to allow for only one form of integration'. Renewed EC expansion and several tiers of integration are likely to force a rethink of the pattern of European institutions and may give individual countries greater flexibility in approaching economic and monetary union. The planned European Central Bank could arguably set monetary conditions for the whole European continent, but could it work effectively with a General Council composed of 30 (or more) central bank governors?

A EUROPEAN ECONOMIC AREA
(WITHOUT AN EMS)

The European Community took a major step forward in formalising improved links with other west European economies in October 1991. The EC and European Free Trade Area countries agreed to create a vast free trade area covering 19 countries, and accounting for almost half of total world trade.

Europe expansion in a nutshell

As we grapple with the complexity of the new European order, let us begin by surveying the suitability of the Community applicants. In terms of population and output the Community accounts for almost all (85 to 90 per cent) of Western Europe.

- The remaining 10 per cent lies within the six countries of the European Free Trade Area in central and northern Europe (dealt with in the next section).
- The countries of Eastern Europe would roughly add a third to Community population, but make a much smaller contribution to total output, perhaps 10 per cent. The minor Baltic States of the former Soviet Union are also pressing for closer EC links.
- Applications from Turkey, Cyprus and Malta point to further EC expansions southward, but these economies are also rather small and are geographically peripheral to the Community.

The European Economic Area has been seen as a stepping stone for the EFTA countries to full Community membership in the mid-1990s. Indeed, the 'no' result of the Swiss referendum on the EEA in December 1992 reflected fears it would inevitably lead to complete integration into the EC. The European Economic Area goes much further than simply removing barriers to free trade. The EFTA countries will adopt EC rules on company law, harmonise their competition policy and allow the free movement of people throughout the EEA. The new European Economic Area thus represents a fast-track to economic integration which may leave Austria on entry more closely linked to the Community economy than Greece after 14 years of full EC membership.

The six EFTA economies are affluent by EC standards.

Table 8.1 National Income per person 1990: EFTA economies

Switzerland	125
Norway	117
Iceland	110
Sweden	108
Finland	105
EC 12	100
Austria	98

Note: EFTA also includes Liechtenstein

This affluence in turn reflects a relatively strong economic performance over the post-war period. Indeed, across a number of indicators — growth, inflation and unemployment — the important EFTA economies have a record which compares favourably with those within the Community. The long-term success of the Swiss central bank in fighting inflation matches that of the Bundesbank, for example, but Switzerland has avoided the high unemployment which beset many of the major EC economies in the 1980s. The entry of the EFTA countries will thus not add to the problems of economic cohesion outlined in the last chapter. Indeed, they will share some of the burden of promoting the economic adjustment required in Spain, Portugal and Greece. The Community will also benefit from the addition of economies which have invested relatively heavily in infrastructure and training.

One potential problem lies in the 'small country' challenge to European decision-making. The inter-governmental committees (such as the European Council) are increasingly taking decisions by qualified voting — each country's vote has a weight which reflects its importance within the Community. However, the votes of the smaller EC Member States tend to carry a disproportionate weight judged on purely economic grounds. The Belgian vote in the Council of Ministers has a weight half that of the German vote, although its national output is only a seventh of the German figure. Table 8.2 illustrates the size of the six EFTA economies relative to the Belgian economy, which in turn accounts for only $3\frac{1}{2}$ per cent of the Community economy:

Table 8.2 The six EFTA economies compared to Belgium

BELGIUM =	100 and 3½% of EC Output
Sweden	97.6
Switzerland	88.2
Austria	75.6
Finland	55.3
Norway	51.4
Iceland	3.0

Based on estimates of national output

If it is proposed that these new Members are also over-represented in the EC decision-making process then the larger countries are likely to find their influence reduced to an unacceptable degree. Unanimous voting which is required in the field of Foreign and Security Policy may also prove unworkable in an expanded Community. There is a danger that the imbalance between rapid progress in economic and monetary union and faltering steps in the creation of pan-European political institutions already evident at Maastricht will be further exacerbated by renewed EC expansion.

EFTA and monetary union

The progress towards a single currency will be given new impetus when the EFTA countries join the Community. Indeed, the majority of these economies already operate explicit currency stabilisation policies and their experience throws light on the broader single currency debate. Figure 8.1 shows the Deutschmark's movements against three European currencies (labelled A, B and C) in the first nine months of 1992. At first glance it is very difficult to identify the Exchange Rate Mechanism member and the two EFTA currencies plotted. In reality, A represents the Italian lira, B the Austrian schilling and C the Swiss franc. Although not a member of the Exchange Rate Mechanism, the credibility of the Austrian currency policy left it unmoved by the currency turbulance which pushed the Deutschmark sharply higher against the Italian lira in the autumn of 1992. The Swiss franc actually gained ground versus the EMS currencies as investors sought a safe home for their funds.

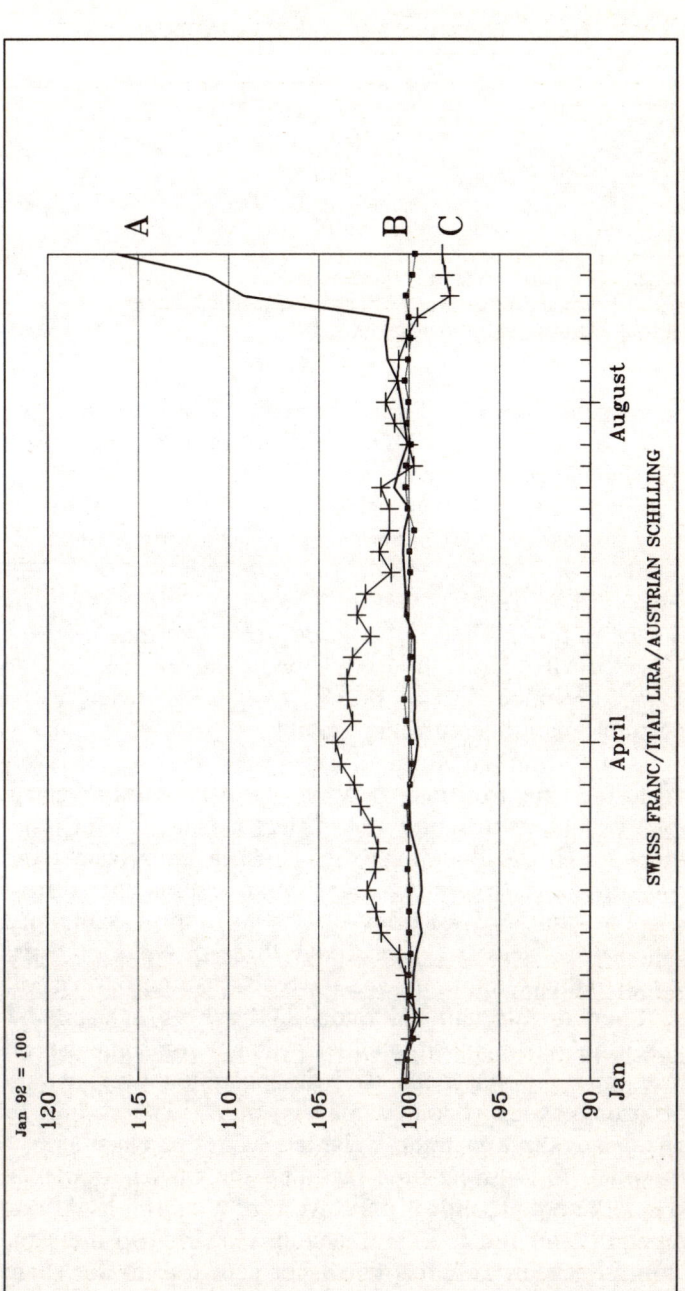

Figure 8.1 Deutschmark — external value against Swiss franc, Italian lira and Austrian schilling, 1992.

Table 8.3 EFTA countries and the Maastricht standards

	Target	Austria	Finland	Iceland	Norway	Sweden	Switzerland
Inflation (%)	$4\frac{1}{4}$	4	$2\frac{3}{4}$	7	$2\frac{1}{2}$	$2\frac{1}{2}$	5
Govt deficit (%)	3	$2\frac{1}{4}$	$7\frac{1}{2}$	$3\frac{1}{2}$	$\frac{1}{2}$	4	2
Govt debt (%)	60	$56\frac{1}{2}$	12	20	-17	$-1\frac{1}{2}$	30
Currency link	ERM	DM	Float	Basket	ECU	ECU	Managed
Long yields (%)	11	$8\frac{1}{4}$	13	$15\frac{1}{2}$	$9\frac{1}{2}$	$9\frac{1}{2}$	7

Govt deficit — as percentage of national output
Govt debt — outstanding debt as percentage of national output
Figures rounded to simplify comparison

The relative fortunes of the Austrian schilling outside the ERM and the Italian lira within it demonstrate the importance of the economic convergence criteria. This evidence also strongly supports the view that while the ERM can help day-to-day currency management, it cannot disguise the impact of economic policy differences. Table 8.3 shows how the EFTA economies stand relative to the Maastricht criteria. Austria meets each of the minimum standards and would thus be ready (along with Switzerland) to join the single currency area at an early stage. Membership of the Exchange Rate Mechanism *alone* cannot guarantee currency stability.

The gains from anchoring exchange rates are positively related to the extent of trade between the economies involved, while an economic structure very different from that of other members raises the potential costs. Austria and Switzerland appear well placed to join the ERM on an assessment of these factors. Two-thirds of Austrian exports go to the Community, with a third to Germany. Just under three-quarters of Swiss exports go to the Community, and the Swiss economy as a whole is very open to international trade. Differences in economic structures do represent a potential problem for some EFTA countries and this has been well demonstrated by Finland's recent problems of currency management. Finland initially linked the markka to a trade-weighted basket of currencies, a basket which for a short time included the Soviet rouble. In mid-1991 this was abandoned in favour of a central ECU rate in preparation for full EC membership. However, in the same year Finnish export volumes fell 8 per cent due to the sharp downturn in Soviet imports and weak forestry exports. Penal interest rates failed to halt flows out of the markka and in November 1991 it was devalued by 12 per cent and in September 1992 allowed to float freely. Norway may face similar problems if the value of its oil exports, a major contributor to national income, were to change dramatically.

Austria and Switzerland have followed very different approaches to currency stabilisation. In contrast to the Austrian schilling's stability against the Deutschmark since 1978, the Swiss franc is a widely traded currency which has fluctuated within a 20 per cent range over this period. The Swiss National Bank looks at a range of indicators, including domestic ones such as money supply growth before setting the level of official interest rates. How badly has the Swiss economic performance and tradable sector been affected by the currency swings?

Economic indicators for Switzerland over the 13 years 1978 to 1990 compare favourably with those for Austria. Growth of both countries has been around $2\frac{1}{4}$ per cent, but unemployment in Switzerland has been neglible over this period. The Swiss inflation figures are better (a 3.1 per cent average against 3.7 per cent in Austria) suggesting that a stable exchange rate is not essential for a successful anti-inflationary policy.

There is little evidence that the currency swings have forced Swiss producers to sell in domestic markets rather than overseas. The proportion of national output exported by the Swiss is 39 per cent, while the comparable figure for Austria is slightly higher at 41 per cent. This is consistent with the models described in Chapter 4 which suggest that a stable exchange rate may promote international trade, but the gains are very modest.

The EFTA economies are likely to be admitted to the Community in the mid-1990s, with the exception of Switzerland whose referendum result will inevitably delay EEA (and EC) entry. Their entry may well create the opportunity for a reworking of the timetable for economic and monetary union. In particular, the condition that a majority of Member States must meet the Maastricht standards before advancing rapidly to Stage Three of EMU is likely to be dropped within an expanded Community. Austria's entry will add to the low inflation and hard currency economies which would form the basis of the single currency area — what has become known as the mini-EMU.

EASTERN EUROPE AND CURRENCY REFORM

Rapid transition to developed market economies in the East European countries requires direct foreign investment and access to markets in the West. This has been recognised by the Community and in December 1991 three East European countries — Hungary, Poland and Czechoslovakia — reached an Association Agreement with the EC. This Agreement gives exports from these countries more favourable treatment with the removal of many quotas and the reduction of tariffs. As with the EFTA accord, progress will be gradual with the target of removing barriers to trade in industrial goods over the next ten years. In this case, however, there is an asymmetry which will help the new Associates by allowing them to delay the steps to liberalising trade. The main problem which faces the former COMECON economies is that they are unable to compete effectively in high value-added product categories. Their concentration on basic industries such as iron and steel leaves them facing the most protected of the Community's industrial sectors. The Czechoslovakian iron and steel industry has already been accused of dumping in EC markets and is threatened with new protectionist measures.

The diversion of trade flows from the Soviet Union to EC Member States has been very rapid for Poland, Hungary and Czechoslovakia. Of Poland's exports in 1991, just under a third went to Germany, more than twice exports to the USSR. Despite the speed of the transformation towards market economies, full Community membership is unlikely before the end of the century. Not only do their industrial structures make full early integration problematic, but their early admittance would add significantly to the disparities in living standards across the Community. Czechoslovakia, for example, is estimated to have a national income per person around the level of Portugal and Greece. In addition, these economies also face a period of dramatic policy adjustment before macroeconomic stability can be achieved. Inflation in 1991 ranged from 35 per cent in Hungary, where it had actually accelerated from the previous year, to 70 per cent in Poland. The absence of sophisticated financial markets has left government revenue short-falls to be met by printing money rather than borrowing.

The domestic problems of controlling inflation must inevitably be reflected in unstable foreign exchange markets. The value of East European currencies have in general proved highly volatile and as a result these currencies have not formed the basis for international trade. An exporter of tractors to a CIS Republic will be wary of accepting roubles if their market value is highly uncertain; indeed the company may be happier holding its tangible output (tractors) than the paper money (roubles). Within this context, trade between former COMECON economies has fallen sharply, and where it does occur is based on barter deals (swapping goods for goods) without involving foreign currencies. The 'currency vacuum' is preventing trade which in a fully developed free market economy would occur.

The result of this trade crisis may be that the first 'ECU zone' will not be centred on Germany and France but on the new Community Associates in Eastern Europe. The ECU could certainly provide a relatively stable unit of account and thus a basis for international transactions. The value of the ECU would still be determined by monetary policy in Western Europe and this would be a guarantee against a sudden loss of value. But how could a country running a temporary current account deficit find the ECUs to meet its import bill? To give the new 'ECU zone' liquidity, foreign central banks or international institutions such as the International Monetary Fund would have to make short-term advances to tide countries over. A recent proposal from the Association for the Monetary Union of Europe argues that a surveillance board would be necessary to ensure that macroeconomic policies in the East European countries are sound. If the ECU proves its worth in international trade perhaps it could be used in domestic transactions as an alternative to the local currency. The United Kingdom's proposal for a 'hard ECU' currency in the Community may have greater applicability in the East.

These ideas for solving the currency crisis in East Europe have close historical parallels. Lenin introduced the chervonet currency in the Soviet Union to circulate alongside the rouble. Its issuance was partially backed by official holdings of gold and it played an important role in the increasingly market-orientated New Economic Policy of the 1920s. More recently, the US dollar was the basis for international trade in Western Europe during the immediate post-war period. The introduction of the ECU in the East would not be a substitute for long-term policy reform, however. Just as the dollar has been replaced by the currencies of the reconstructed Japanese and German economies in recent decades, if all goes well the ECU will finally be redundant.

ANOTHER SOUTHWARD EXPANSION?

The relatively favourable economic performance of countries such as Spain and Portugal since accession has spurred new applications. In 1987 Turkey submitted its application, to be followed by Cyprus and Malta in 1990. The Community governments have been keen not to neglect Turkey's application but any hopes of early full membership are misplaced. It is more likely that these three economies will follow the same path as those of Eastern Europe, with an extended period of Association and gradual integration into the broader EEA trading area.

CONCLUSIONS: EFTA, COMECON AND ALL THAT

- The European Community is now faced with a major challenge in not only deepening integration but also broadening to include other European economies.
- Members of the European Free Trade Area are included in a 19-country European Economic Area. The experience of the EFTA countries demonstrates that currency stability can be achieved outside the ERM, and that such stability has only a modest advantage in promoting trade.
- The Associate status of the East European economies makes full membership unlikely until the end of the decade, but the ECU could play an important role in facilitating international trade in the East.

The torrent of applications to join the Community has been motivated by a number of factors, but important among them are pure economic considerations associated with access to the EC's affluent markets. From the perspective of a small trading economy, world trade is increasingly dominated by regional trading blocs and the new European Economic Area will be the largest of these. The Community's place in global trade patterns and the advantages associated with a single currency are discussed in Chapter 9.

Chapter
NINE

THE ECU BLOC IN A THREE-BLOC WORLD?

●●●

THREE-BLOC WORLD

On the evening of 20 September 1992, television reporters roamed Paris asking French voters in the Maastricht referendum which way they had voted and why. Rather than narrow economic calculation, it was clear that broad themes had dominated: a fear of losing national identity and, for the 'oui' voters, a belief that a united Europe would be a world power to match the United States and Japan. It is the external benefits of a single currency which prompted Jacques Delors to write that: 'If you are not a European, read about the ECU with care, for it will be a world currency to rival the dollar and the yen'.

Any re-think of the European approach to economic and monetary union must take into account the global context for these decisions. With the relative decline of the United States as an economic power and the end of the Cold War, world economic relations are becoming increasingly dominated by regional trade agreements. New economic empires are being established based not on conquest but mutual co-operation. Indeed, it has been argued that we are heading for a 'three-bloc world'.

Respecting the sensitivities of the other Community members, in this text the European zone will be referred to as the 'ECU bloc' rather than the 'DMark bloc'. The benefits on the global stage of establishing this ECU bloc can be divided into two broad categories: those deriving from the EC as a major free

The three-bloc world

- the DMark/ECU bloc — taking in the new European Economic Area and eventually Eastern Europe
- the dollar bloc — the United States, Canada, Mexico and ultimately the whole of South America.
- the yen bloc — Japan and the South East Asian economies.

trade area, and those deriving from the ECU as a currency of global standing. The arguments that Europe must enhance its role as a regional trade association are the most convincing and to these we turn first.

THE FATE OF URUGUAY

Whatever happened to GATT?

International trade during the inter-war period had been characterised by protectionist pressures and bilateral trade disputes, and this contributed to a sharp contraction in trade during the 1930s Depression. In the hope of avoiding these mistakes, the General Agreement on Tariffs and Trade was established to provide a multilateral framework — measures to liberalise trade followed rounds of negotiations involving all countries. This approach incorporated a major principle of non-discrimination between trading partners. If Germany gave a trade concession to France, for example, then the rules meant that these concessions must be extended to all other countries (they are accorded Most-Favoured-Nation status). This gave an important protection to small open economies which in negotiating with the major trading nations on a bilateral basis would be rather like David confronted by Goliath. The commitment of the Western powers to free trade and the success of the GATT system led to a substantial reduction in barriers to trade.

The world of international trade negotiators is dominated by 'isms'. Over recent decades the multilateralism formula has been gradually replaced by a new regionalism. Europe has been at the heart of this development from the beginning. The 1957 Treaty of Rome laid the foundation for the Common Market, and was quickly followed by an agreement on the European Free Trade Area. The EEC was welcomed as a healthy part of the post-war reconstruction in Europe and the GATT rules permitted the formation of regional trade areas as long as trade barriers were not increased for outsiders. There was no immediate defensive response from Europe's trading partners and with world trade growing at a satisfactory rate the multi-lateral approach to trade appeared intact.

The more difficult economic environment of the 1970s and 1980s reinforced protectionist pressures and brought a regional dimension to US trade policy. The United States and Canada signed a Free Trade Agreement at the beginning of 1988 creating a unified market of 275 million consumers. August 1992 brought 'NAFTA', an agreement between the United States, Mexico and Canada to remove tariffs and quotas over the next 15 years. This pact creates a market of 360 million consumers and a total output of 6 trillion dollars. And how large will the yen block be? Unfortunately, the final piece of the 'three-block' jigsaw doesn't quite fall into place. Japanese links with its South East Asian neighbours in trade and direct investment have been growing rapidly, but these have yet to be cemented with a regional trade accord. Japan has a clear interest in free inter-regional trade, as the United States represents a major export market while its East Asian neighbours remain suspicious of Japanese-led regional trade initiatives. The members of the Association of South East Asian Nations (including Indonesia, Malaysia, Singapore and Thailand among others) have taken tentative steps toward creating a trade area but progress is likely to be slow.

Free trade or fortress trade?

In this developing two-bloc world are outsiders faced with 'Fortress Europe' and 'Fortress America'? Studies of the extent to which the new blocs have created higher external trade walls than the average for the individual members come up with mixed results. GATT has reviewed the US–Canada agreement but has failed to find conclusive evidence that the agreement raised trade barriers for outsiders. In Europe, for example, Spain reduced tariffs from 13 per cent to 5 per cent in certain industrial sectors when it adopted the Community standards. However, along with Portugal, Spain significantly increased its protection for agriculture products under the umbrella of the Common Agricultural Policy. Even where the external trade barriers of the region are no higher than those prevailing before the agreement outside suppliers can still lose out. As the new structure of tariffs discriminates between trading partners, consumers may end up buying from suppliers from another country within the free trade area even if they are less efficient than external producers.

The reduced role for multilateralism is immediately evident in the current Uruguay round of GATT negotiations. An IMF report concludes that 'Smaller countries would be the most hurt by a drift towards regionalism that undermines the principle of ... non-discrimination' and as a defensive measure the unattached developing countries, recognising this threat, are also coalescing into regional interest groups. The negotiations are increasingly dominated by economic blocs relatively closed to overseas trade (US/Canada export only 7 per cent of national output) and the impetus for multilateral agreement appears to have been lost. Preparations for the Uruguay round were begun in 1982, negotiations in 1986, and there is currently optimism that agreement will be reached before the end of 1993. For the European nations this failure of multilateralism may, in some respects, be a favourable development. The Community now speaks with a single voice and carries the weight of the whole trading bloc — the European Economic Area. France has used the negotiating muscle of the entire EC to defend its agricultural interests, but the role of the individual nation state looks increasingly marginalised.

TRADING BLOCS — THE CURRENCY INGREDIENT

But this book is about the European Exchange Rate Mechanism not the rather dull world of international trade negotiations. What plans do the Americans have for introducing a North American dollar in Canada and Mexico? Is the United States central bank, the Federal Reserve, de facto running monetary

Table 9.1   Growth of trade within and outside regions

$ billion	1980	1989	Growth (%)
European Community			
Total exports	691.2	1133.7	64.0
Exports to rest of world	322.2	455.9	41.5
Trade within region	369.1	677.8	83.6
North America			
Total exports	304.1	509.2	67.4
Exports to rest of world	204.6	303.9	48.5
Trade within region	99.5	205.3	106.3
South East Asia			
Total exports	283.1	641.4	126.6
Exports to rest of world	186.8	417.8	123.7
Trade within region	96.4	223.6	132.0

Source: J. J. Schott — Trading Blocs and the World Trading System

policy throughout the Continent? The answers are none and no. Nor are the Japanese quaking at the prospect of ECUs circulating in Belgium. With freely floating exchange rates, influence in the geopolitical arena is largely related to economic strength (however defined) rather than to currency and monetary issues. The North American Free Trade Agreement does set up a supra-national body but its role is limited to settling trade disputes alongside the GATT procedures. There is no North American equivalent of Jacques Delors and with Mexico now within the NAFTA umbrella reference to the 'dollar bloc' is clearly a misnomer.

Canada — on the edge of the dollar union

Canada, in particular, seems to do just as well as Switzerland in dealing with floating exchange rates. Canada is a relatively small economy set alongside a huge monetary union — the United States — and thus may serve as a model for European countries unwilling or unable to join in the initial Single Currency Area.

The degree of integration between Canadian and United States manufacturing industries (and particularly in car production) is exceptionally high, despite volatility in the currency markets. The United States takes three-quarters of Canadian exports and provides two-thirds of its imports. A manufacturing process may be started in the United States, and then the partly finished goods shipped across the border for completion in Canada. The greater part of the Canadian industrial base lies in relatively close proximity to the US border.

As the US economy is ten times the size of its neighbour, policy changes in the US inevitably have a major impact on the Canadian economic outlook. Canadian economic autonomy is carefully guarded within this constraint and interest rates are set with the primary objective of containing *domestic* inflation, although naturally exchange rate developments quickly feed through into domestic prices. Just as with dollar/DMark rates, there is considerable month-to-month volatility in the Canadian–US dollar exchange rate along with pronounced trend moves away from the levels suggested by Purchasing Power Parity. This volatility has been enhanced by the constitutional reform associated with French-speaking Quebec — a mirror image of the German reunification shock. Indeed, the Canadian–US dollar rate first fell through par in 1976 with the victory of the Parti Quebecois in that province. A substantial interest rate differential with the United States would have been required if parity had been the central rate of a North American ERM. As for the relative inflation performances, over the 30 years to 1990, US inflation averaged 5.1 per cent, and that of Canada was fractionally higher at 5.5 per cent.

THE ECU'S GLOBAL ROLE

Will the growth of Europe's influence as a trading area be matched by the ascendancy of the ECU? It is already playing a greater role in the European bond markets (outlined in Chapter 4) and may eventually become a form of 'international money' in a global, not just a European, context. Just as prices across Europe are easier to compare if expressed in ECUs rather than various national currencies, there is a parallel need for a widely recognised global unit of account in integrated international markets, such as those for commodities. The dollar is now the currency for pricing many commodities throughout the world; petroleum companies will be comparing the dollar per barrel price of oil from the North Sea with the dollar per barrel price of oil from Kuwait. Commodity pricing is just one aspect of the dollar's dominance as an 'international money'. Studies of the pattern of international trade show that in the late 1980s just under half of foreign trade invoicing was in US dollars. When private individuals and companies decide to hold foreign currencies, on average, the dollar will account for half the total. For central banks the weighting in favour of the US currency is even more pronounced.

But the times they are a-changing in the world of international finance, just as they have for international trade. The United States isn't the economic power it once was and its importance in international trade is rather overshadowed by the European Economic Area. In any case the dollar hasn't been doing its job. Ideally, the 'international money' should hold its value reasonably well, but since the 1960s the greenback has depreciated by two-thirds against both the Deutschmark and the yen. The economist, Ricardo wrote that 'A currency to be perfect, should be absolutely invariable in value'. Holders of non-interest bearing dollar accounts or the paper bills themselves, who have lost out through US inflation, might well agree. Policy-makers in small countries have increasingly turned to alternatives to the devalued dollar as a basis for their exchange rate policies. In 1975 roughly half the IMF currencies were pegged to the dollar, but by 1990 this had dropped to only a quarter.

The European currencies have been favoured by the shift away from the dollar, the Deutschmark in particular. It is argued that the ECU, following monetary union, may be as important as the dollar or perhaps be *the* international money in the 21st Century. Certainly the plans for an independent European Central Bank committed to low inflation suggest it will keep its value better than the dollar. The current pattern of international trade and prospective developments in Eastern Europe both point to a major international role for the ECU.

It turns out that the direct benefits to Europeans of this 'external dimension' to monetary union are likely to be rather modest, however. If a loan from an American bank to a South African mining company is denominated in ECUs rather than dollars this doesn't have an impact on European living standards. The European Commission survey of the benefits from monetary union has identified the following areas of potential benefit:

- The ECU's increased use in trade invoicing and financial markets will reduce the currency risk in dealing with non-Community countries and open the way for European banks to operate in their home currency.
- Overseas holdings of ECUs in cash will represent an interest-free loan to the European governments.

In total, however, these gains will not amount to more than 0.1 per cent of Community national output and will thus be relatively small compared to the internal benefits from free trade or a single currency. Certainly the international pattern is for the development of free trade, not single currency, areas.

For the moment, among the European currencies the Deutschmark has the leading role. On a typical day dollar/DMark trading will account for a third of total business in the New York currency market and a fifth of the business in London. A detailed analysis of price changes in the foreign exchange markets suggests that this dollar–DMark axis (sometimes referred to as dollar–DMark polarity) creates problems in managing the European Monetary System which monetary union would help to solve. The September 1992 ERM crisis followed a rather familiar pattern as during the summer months the dollar had been under general downward pressure as economic growth in the United States proved disappointing. Empirically, dollar weakness tends to favour the Deutschmark to a greater degree than the other ERM currencies and thus intensifies pressures for realignments. Attempts to explain this have looked at capital controls and differences in transaction costs but on the whole the explanations have proved unsatisfactory. Whatever the cause, a greater weight for the ECU in international wealth holding may well reduce the significance of these dollar-related shocks to the ERM.

G7 AND THE UNITED EUROPE

In contrast to the increased regionalism of the trade negotiations, policy co-ordination remains dominated by the concerns of individual nations. Germany, Italy, France and the United Kingdom each have individual representations at the Group of Seven summits to discuss world economic progress. Their contributions often reflect national concerns rather than pan-European economic developments. Indeed, the summits in the first half of 1992 brought calls both from the United States and Community countries for Germany to consider lowering interest rates.

Would monetary union in Europe improve global economic co-ordination and give the EC a greater say? Certainly the increased convergence called for by the Maastricht Treaty makes a combined European voice more likely. There has already been a tendency at times of crisis for the main deals to be struck by an inner core of countries — the United States, Japan and Germany. A single EC representation could well lead to speedier decision-making without marginalising the smaller Community countries. But the gains at this global level of cooperation will only be made if the European decision-making process itself proves to be effective. All the national central banks are represented on the General Council of the European Central Banks and responsibility for exchange rate policy is shared in turn with the European Council. Ultimately, the internal and external aspects of monetary union are linked. If the single currency area is giving the right internal results and a consensus can be achieved, it brings the opportunity to exercise a powerful European influence on global decision-making. If not, there is immense scope for policy disarray.

CONCLUSIONS: THE ECU BLOC IN A THREE-BLOC WORLD

- There is mounting evidence that the world economy is being dominated by regional economic zones, primarily based on trade agreements.
- In international trade, regionalism has dealt a powerful blow to the principle of multilateralism and left small open economies increasingly exposed.
- European monetary integration would give the ECU a major role in international monetary affairs, but the direct benefits to Europe of this development are modest.
- A single European voice in global policy discussions could promote co-ordination. This strong external voice is dependent on the effective internal operation of the new pan-European institutions.

Part
FOUR

DOES EMU HAVE A FUTURE?

THE OUTLOOK FOR A SINGLE CURRENCY

UNPREDICTABLE TIMES — THE FUTURE AND THE FINANCIAL MARKETS

The 1992 currency crisis represented a threat to the European approach to foreign exchange management, but also an opportunity. The threat was clear, as the crisis had dark historical parallels. Massive international capital flows swept away central bank attempts to contain downward pressure on the lira and sterling, making even an orderly realignment perilous. The disarray in the currency markets was likened by a veteran German central banker to the final days of the Bretton Woods system. The eventual temporary suspension of the two currencies was also reminiscent of the ill-fated 1970s 'Snake' of European currencies, which France left, rejoined, and then abandoned for good.

If the crisis was simply the product of an irrational herd instinct in the currency markets, then as the London *Financial Times* had it 'Only dealers won in lira support'. Hopefully, the arguments of this book convince the reader that the currency pressures were symptoms of underlying economic divergences, which the Exchange Rate Mechanism after Maastricht was ill-placed to resist. Some elements of the system came out stronger for the test, the Belgian franc/Deutschmark rate barely flickered and the French franc was successfully defended. But the opportunity lies in the future — using the lessons of this crisis to help shape a more appropriate approach to currency management for Europe in the 1990s.

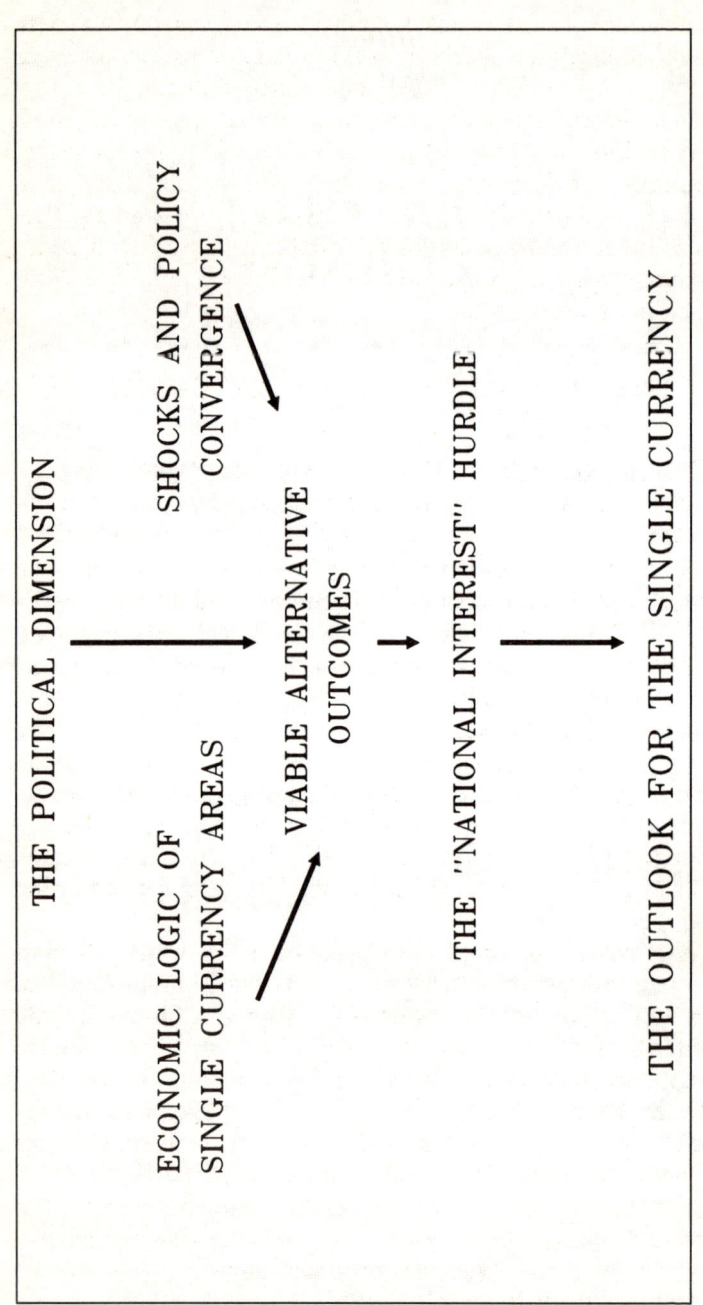

Figure 10.1 European and monetary union

In looking forward to the next five or ten years of foreign exchange policy, three background influences must be assessed (see Figure 10.1). The 'viable' alternative outcomes for the Exchange Rate Mechanism are then to be considered, and judged against the pattern of national economic interests in the Community. An approach to monetary union failing to meet with the Bundesbank's approval would be a non-starter. The scenario judged most likely for the Exchange Rate Mechanism and monetary union (based on a twin-exchange rate régime) is outlined in greatest detail.

THE POLITICS OF MONETARY UNION

Political confidence in the EC institutions and the path toward monetary union are closely intertwined. The European Central Bank and an ECU area must not be created as an initial, short-lived experiment in powerful European institutions. The primary focus of this book has been on the economic context of the ERM debate, but there are three political concepts which will bear directly on the ECU's fate.

- subsidiarity;
- a multi-speed Europe;
- a Europe of multi-dimensional integration.

Subsidiarity

The increased significance of 'subsidiarity' for Europe will tend to postpone the broad application of the final stages of monetary union. The European Monetary System with occasional realignments devolves control over monetary policy to the lowest level (the national central banks) while facilitating a pan-European approach to management of currency fluctuations. However, for the countries faced with a high degree of economic inter-dependence at the core of Europe, this is clearly insufficient. Even in the light of subsidiarity, there are strong grounds for arguing that a mini-EMU Central Bank is required. Only in this way will the concerns of the smaller economies be reflected in the single currency area's monetary policy.

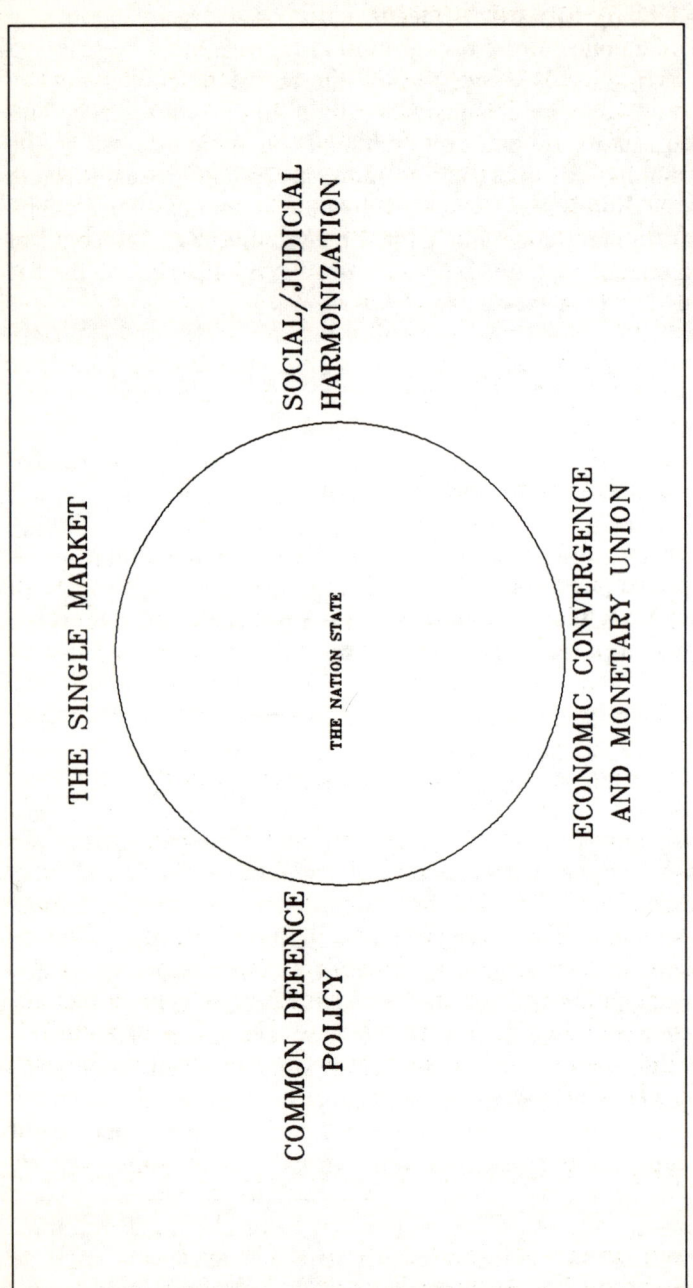

Figure 10.2 Multi-dimensional integration

The multi-speed Europe

The concept of a two-speed Europe may already be out-dated just as it is being advanced as a solution to the problems posed by the ERM crisis. The accession of Greece, Spain and Portugal has already contributed considerably to the diversity of the Community and special arrangements have allowed them to adjust slowly in certain areas to pan-European norms. The plans to broaden membership further not just to the EFTA countries but Eastern Europe will no doubt mean additional 'speeds' in Community harmonization. A multi-speed approach to monetary union thus lies within the general direction of Community developments rather than leading a new and potentially hazardous way forward.

The multiple-choice Europe

The scope of Community issues is gradually widening as the 'European Economic Community' develops into a deeper 'European Union'. The Maastricht Treaty lays the foundation for increased co-operation in social policy and defence issues. This broadening came at the cost of diluting the assumption that, whatever speed individual Member states were proceeding at, they were all heading for the same objective. The United Kingdom not only doesn't have to comply with the agreement on social policy for the moment, it doesn't agree in principle. The accommodation of the Community to the concerns of the Danish people at the Edinburgh Summit also suggests that increased flexibility will be allowed for individual Member States. Each State's integration with the Community will be mapped out across several dimensions (see Figure 10.2) and monetary union will only be one of these. Replacing a national currency with the ECU bearing Jacques Delors' head is unlikely to be the sole test of commitment to the European Union even in the 21st Century.

THE ECONOMICS OF MONETARY UNION

Overlaid on the political backdrop is the 'economic logic' of adopting the ECU — the main subject of this book. It was clear from our discussion in Chapter 4 that major economic benefits are to be had from reducing barriers to trade and mobility within the Community — not creating a single currency area. Only very volatile exchange rates (adjusted for inflation) dampen trade. Substantial progress has already been made in implementing the Community Directives to create a single market, but start-1993 represents a staging-post in this process, not the final destination. The additional steps are likely to be increasingly politically sensitive for the Community member states and require lengthy negotiation. With much of the single market task ahead of European governments, not behind them, the economics of the situation point to greater emphasis on a deepening of trade integration over the next five years rather than a major revolution in European monetary institutions. Indeed, the divisions within the Community created by the ERM debacle suggest that too rapid progress toward a pan-European currency area could damage other areas of European co-operation.

Exchange rates aren't just a barometer of prudence in economic policy with short-term stability against the Deutschmark as some sort of holy grail. Currency pressures reflect shocks to individual Member States (such as German reunification) and changes in the exchange rate can act as a 'safety-valve' until wages and other domestic prices adjust. Countries built on a federal structure (such as the United States) can do without the safety valve but federal budget transfers cushion the blows to individual states. Over the next five years, Europe is unlikely to have the federal budget, the labour mobility or the wage flexibility to adopt the ECU as a pan-European currency. But there are substantial differences in the extent of economic integration and in the likelihood of country-specific shocks for the individual Community economies. The economic logic points to a multi-tier approach to monetary union, with a core of closely linked economies at the centre.

The European Monetary System was set up very much as the *modus operandi* of day-to-day currency management. Its major institutional innovations related to intervention-finance and the framework for agreeing realignments. But the Maastricht Treaty gave a new gloss to the ERM, suggesting that devaluations should become increasingly infrequent as the establishment of the single currency area is approached.

Anchoring exchange rates and foregoing realignments represents very much a 'rule-based' approach to economic policy co-ordination, one in which monetary policy autonomy inevitably migrates from the weak currency to the hard currency central banks. It is the Bundesbank which in the end is primarily determining inflation in the ECU (or is it Deutschmark?) currency bloc. The policy tensions between the United Kingdom and Germany ahead of sterling's departure from the System are thus inherent in the post-Maastricht operation of the System.

There is clearly a case for institutional reform within the ERM if we are to stick with the original plan of gradually edging toward monetary union. Accepting Bundesbank decisions unquestioningly over the next five years without representation on its Council will not be a problem for some central banks — for them it is only the Bundesbank's record in containing inflation which makes the Deutschmark a suitable anchor. But other European central banks have achieved their own anti-inflationary credibility (the Swiss National Bank for one) while retaining exchange rate flexibility. For them membership of an unreformed ERM would represent an unacceptable loss of policy sovereignty.

ECONOMIC SHOCKS AND POLICY DIVERGENCE IN THE 1990S

Economic reforms are largely a product of their times rather than political or economic theorising. It was the cost of the Cold War which contributed to the downfall of the Bretton Woods fixed exchange rate system in the early 1970s, rather than academic articles by the economist Milton Friedman. It was the cost of the end of the Cold War which shook the Exchange Rate Mechanism, not newspaper articles by Alan Walters. What potential shocks will influence the development of the Mechanism in the 1990s?

As far as we can tell, the world economic environment should be gradually improving in the next few years. 1991 was the first year of contraction in world output since the Second World War, with growth in the developed market economies also proving relatively sluggish at only 0.8 per cent. Consensus estimates suggest that this dip in growth will prove short-lived but there is considerable uncertainty surrounding the timing of the rebound. Economic expansion in the major economies should gradually accelerate in 1993, fuelled by lower interest rates in the United States and more generous budget policies in some other countries. The internationally respected fore-caster, the OECD*, expects growth to be running close to $2\frac{1}{2}$ per cent by mid-1994. In Western Europe, growth is likely to be a little slower than this and pan-European unemployment may well continue rising to reach a peak of $10\frac{1}{2}$ per cent in mid-1993. On balance, the general economic environment for Community policy-makers is unlikely to improve significantly until 1994.

Convergence in the community?

The waning impact of divergent economic shocks within Europe, however, may contribute to stability within the Exchange Rate Mechanism.

- For Germany: The boom days for the German economy are over and the lurch toward a more expansionary fiscal policy over recent years looks set to be reversed. If plans to reduce German borrowing are implemented, perhaps through higher income taxes, the Bundesbank has made it clear this will open the way to a more pronounced easing in Deutschmark interest rates. Overall economic growth and the German policy mix will move closer to the Community average.

- For the United Kingdom: The effective devaluation of sterling and lower interest rates look set to promote economic growth, although this rebound will be hampered by high personal debt levels. In

* The Organisation for Economic Co-operation and Development regularly prepares economic projections for the developed market economies.

1991, German growth exceeded that in the United Kingdom by a full 5 per cent — in 1994 the UK's growth could be slightly higher. Given the disinflationary forces already at work in the economy, sterling weakness is unlikely to significantly boost domestic inflation.

- For Italy: There is now much greater uncertainty over its prospects following this summer's political crisis. However, there have been encouraging signs that the currency crisis will trigger domestic economic reform. The scala mobile wage-indexation agreement has finally been abandoned, and the Amato government's plans to reduce the budget deficit have met with parliamentary approval. Inflation data for early 1993 indicate the lira's sharp losses have not pushed inflation above the 6 per cent of recent years.

On balance, the economic pressures which have contributed to the ERM crisis are likely to ease, providing a window of opportunity in the mid-1990s for sterling and lira re-entry at new, more sustainable central rates. It is most unlikely that the ERM would demand a British monetary policy excessively tight on purely domestic grounds under these circumstances.

There are two major uncertainties surrounding the outlook. The first lies with the Maastricht standards for the single currency area. A sharp shift toward tighter pan-European monetary and fiscal policy could occur if all countries try to hit the targets simultaneously. This now looks less likely in the wake of the ERM crisis, but such a development might prevent the world economic recovery gathering momentum. The second major uncertainty lies with former-East Germany and the other transitional economies in Eastern Europe. There is mounting evidence that the production cut-backs of the transitional economies are largely at an end but high unemployment could well lead to renewed social disorder there. Paradoxically, instability in Eastern Europe may help the ERM as renewed refugee inflows into Germany would undermine the Deutschmark's 'safe-haven status', making alternatives (such as the FFr) more attractive to investors.

THE ERM ALTERNATIVES AND THE NATIONAL INTERESTS

Figure 10.3 shows some of the alternative ways in which the Exchange Rate Mechanism could develop in the wake of the 1992 Crisis. These will be reviewed in the light of national interests and a verdict delivered on the likelihood (and indeed desirability) of these developments. To prevent the analysis becoming too complex, the European economies can be grouped together to reflect their relative standing, for the purposes of this discussion:

- The 'core' countries are Germany, France and the Benelux states. The Benelux currencies trade in a very narrow range against the Deutschmark, the anchor for the Exchange Rate Mechanism. France gains core status having developed a closer relationship with the Bundesbank during the September 1992 crisis and because of its importance to European integration in the broader scheme of things.
- The fringe 'core' countries are Denmark and Ireland. Currencies trade within narrow ERM bands but their presence is not necessary to the development of a single currency area. The result of the Danish referendum and the close trading relations between Ireland and the UK undermine their positions as key core currencies.
- The flexible-link countries are Spain, Portugal, the United Kingdom and Italy.
- The hard-currency non-Community countries are Austria, Switzerland and most of Scandinavia.

Each of the possible outcomes must satisfy enough of the Community (or at least the key ERM players) enough of the time to be sustainable.

The free-float

The possibility that the ERM breaks up altogether and European currencies float freely (as they do within the North

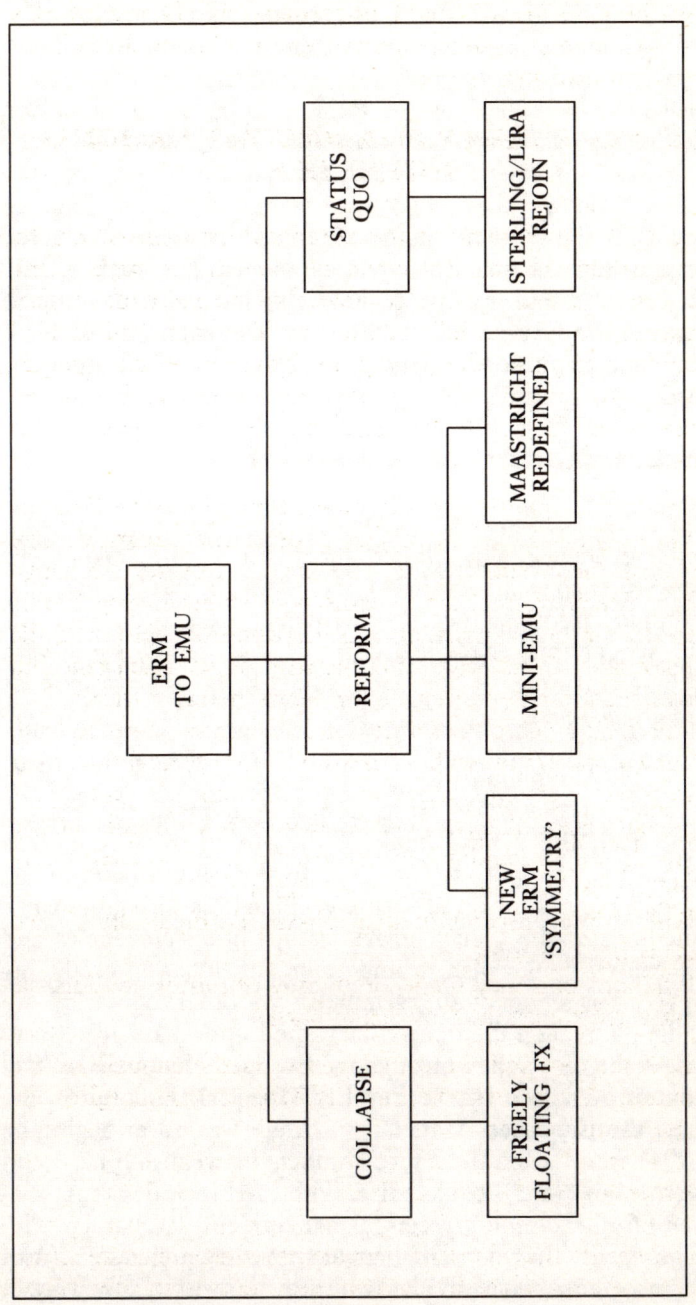

Figure 10.3 The outlook for monetary union

American Free Trade Area) can be dismissed quickly. The close economic links between the Benelux economies and that of Germany reduce the pressures for currency-adjustment and increase the potential cost of foreign exchange instability on trade flows. For France, the break-up of the ERM would strike at the heart of progress toward a monetary union, and the 'franc-fort' policy is likely to remain at the heart of its economic policy. Even if a franc devaluation is forced by speculative flows, France would act quickly to restore momentum to the EMU process. An end to the ERM could also have an unfavourable impact on the flexible-link economies. The external discipline of the Maastricht convergence standards would be diluted, or indeed, entirely lost.

ERM and Maastricht reinterpreted

If the ERM is to survive, in what form will this be and with which currencies? The United Kingdom, in the wake of its temporary suspension of ERM membership, has argued that institutional reform is necessary. Indeed, there is a consensus in the Community that the European Monetary System, with the dominant role of the Deutschmark, is not working as originally planned.

A new 'ERM' symmetry

The rules of the ERM were designed to make the System symmetrical; the central bank of the strongest currency has an equal responsibility to intervene to the central bank of the weak currency. The Bundesbank's willingness to countenance revaluations of the Deutschmark against other currencies and other central banks wish to import its anti-inflation credibility however, has created an asymmetry. If other countries are unwilling to realign their currencies, the Bundesbank is de facto setting monetary policy throughout Europe. This problem will ultimately be solved by the European Central Bank but in the interim the European Monetary Institute (set up at beginning of 1994) could arbitrate where conflicts between the hard and soft-currency central banks arise. The EMI includes representatives of all Community central bankers and is charged with strengthening 'the co-ordination of monetary policies ... with the aim of ensuring price stability'. In this new framework it would have judged whether the primary responsibility for preventing sterling/DMark dropping out of its ERM band lay with the Bank of England or the Bundesbank. Technical changes to the intervention rules within the European Monetary System wouldn't help much. It is the underlying policy conflicts which need resolving.

This raises a problem for the Bundesbank. It jealously guards its autonomy and argues that the Deutschmark's role as an anchor for the ERM has been a useful one, encouraging low inflation throughout the Community. However, the impact on the German money supply of the 1992 ERM crisis demonstrates that it also has an interest in an *orderly* system of currency management. With many European central banks still under direct government control, the Bundesbank is unlikely to cede autonomy to the EMI. However, it may agree to work (at its discretion) with the EMI* in resolving ERM strains and the underlying policy conflicts. Certainly the prospects for European unemployment out to 1995 indicate the ERM will continue to be criticised for its deflationary bias in the next few years, thus enhancing the pressure for this type of ERM reform.

For the flexible-link countries, they remain on nominal equal status with those of the core and continue to play a role in monetary co-ordination. There is no formal disenfranchisement which could occur with the early development of a formal mini-EMU.

The mini-EMU
Are we on the verge of a new central bank for the ERM core countries? It has been argued that the 1992 ERM crisis made clear the dangers of too long a monetary engagement, and the advantages of an early union. Let's put the currency speculators out of business once and for all with a single currency for the core countries. The creation of the 'ECCB' — the European Core Central Bank — would mean the Bundesbank giving up control of monetary conditions in Germany. On the other hand, some of the core states currently have a better inflation

---

* The Maastricht Treaty already specifies that: 'The EMI shall . . . normally be consulted by the national monetary authorities before they take decisions on the course of monetary policy in the context of *ex ante* co-ordination'.

performance than Germany itself and their central banks are judged to have acted more responsibly. It brings a tangible symbol of European integration (the ECU) much closer and thus may be favoured by the Euro-enthusiasts. All the core countries now have a say in setting European interest rates rather than taking orders from Frankfurt. The flexible-link countries are left to float outside the inner core unless they finally decide to join on the original members' terms.

However, actually circulating ECUs rather than national currencies is a dramatic institutional change which will face opposition even among those who favour stable currencies. Polls in Germany consistently suggest that three-quarters favour retention of the Deutschmark. Indeed, there are intermediate measures which can enhance stability at the centre, without involving the ECU. A further narrowing of the ERM bands (say to $+/-\frac{1}{2}$ per cent) for the core countries would underline the authorities' commitment to fixed exchange rates. The central banks retain ultimate control over their respective monetary policies as national currencies are still in circulation. A specific forum for policy co-ordination could be established at the same time as the bands are narrowed. This leaves the Franco–German alliance at the forefront of European monetary integration, as it has been for economic integration and defence. A less formal alternative would be simply to develop de facto closer co-operation in the context of the EMI and other Community institutions.

Maastricht reinterpreted

The potential rush for convergence among the ERM economies was one of the most dangerous potential results of the Treaty. This is unfair on the Treaty as it involves an inherently flexible timetable for convergence, with scope for late joiners, and allows for ERM devaluations as long as they are not initiated by the central bank concerned. It has largely been a matter of interpretation which has created problems for the Exchange Rate Mechanism, as national politicians attempted to keep the pro-convergence momentum going. The November 1992 devaluations of the peseta and escudo suggest that the ERM is once again being viewed as a system of adjustable central rates — not of fixed exchange rates.

For the Bundesbank and the other core members the

Maastricht standards play an important role in defining the nature of the single currency area. For the flexible-link economies, they provide a target for pro-convergence economic planning. To abandon them would meet with disfavour throughout the EC. However, it may also become more widely accepted that the Community's Maastricht commitment to 'enter swiftly into the third stage' of monetary union, will inevitably create a single currency area excluding some of the major economies. Indeed, being one of the founder members of the ECU zone carries with it few advantages as the terms for additional members have been laid out in advance. The 'rush to convergence' may well be called off and Community-wide monetary union consigned to some distant undefined date.

The status quo *ex ante* revisited

Suppose the lira rejoins in mid-1993, perhaps with a 6 per cent band, followed by sterling later that year. Our analysis of the economic shocks and policy divergence within the Community certainly points to a window of opportunity for this. Can the status quo *ex ante* be established as we quickly forget the market madness of September 1992? The core countries seem willing to permit the re-entry as long as the returning countries obey the rules. Indeed, they would regard it as healthy that the rest of Europe is back on the low-inflation/budget prudence track. However, the re-entry is likely to be at lower exchange rates and thus represents a devaluation for sterling and the lira. In addition the impetus toward early monetary union has been lost and the value of periodic currency adjustments amply demonstrated. An ERM very similar to the one sterling and the lira temporarily quit, may prove more flexible for this reason.

THE OUTLOOK FOR A SINGLE CURRENCY

- The core of ERM currencies (including the French franc) tighten their ERM trading ranges and the central banks announce a more formal but *non-binding* forum for monetary policy. With the establishment of the European Monetary Institute at the beginning of 1994, this then becomes the primary point for pan-European monetary co-operation.

■ Other currencies retain their current bands and both Britain and Italy return with broader +/−6 per cent ranges shortly after the establishment of the EMI in January. There are periodic realignments for these currencies.

■ The new States joining the Community in the mid-1990s enter both currency streams. Austria is rapidly absorbed into the core, with other EFTA currencies in the flexible link area.

■ By the turn of the century, the European Union consists of two currency regimes. At its heart an ECU zone with a single currency area and a European Central Bank. Other currencies are linked to the ECU, with defined trading ranges, but in response to a country-specific economic shock may choose to realign.

■ The distinction between Community review of monetary and fiscal policies in the Maastricht Treaty is dropped. Divergent monetary and fiscal policies among the flexible-link group leave the country concerned open to Community wrath.

■ European Community budgetary revenues will have expanded significantly by the year 2000 but remain insufficient to make all currency adjustments unnecessary.

CONCLUSION

The economic arguments tell you that there are advantages in having a single currency for foreign trade and in disciplining economic policy. But currency rigidity can also increase short-term instability when economies are hit by particular shocks, such as German reunification. On balance for many Community countries there is no *compelling* reason to progress toward a single currency. The primary motivation for adopting this goal may thus be political, with the ECU note as a clear symbol that a new single state is being created. The debate on the single currency area thus draws on many of the central themes of the more general debate about Europe's future. The Delors Report on economic and monetary union makes a direct reference to plurality in the Community. In the case of monetary policy, the question is, should the plurality of national currencies be built-in or ironed out? A Community with a twin-exchange rate regime, based around a central ECU core, will be better placed to respond to the needs of both new applicants and existing Members.

THE ECU COMPOSITION

• •

Deutschmark	0.6242
French franc	1.332
Sterling	0.08784
Netherlands guilder	0.2198
Italian lira	151.8
Belgian franc	3.301
Danish krone	0.1976
Greek drachma	1.440
Irish punt	0.008552
Luxembourg franc	0.130
Spanish peseta	6.885
Portugese escudo	1.393

(Currency units per ecu)

THE ERM PRE-MAASTRICHT: REALIGNMENTS AND PARTICIPATION
(All re-alignments versus ECU)

• •

Mar 1979	BELGIAN FRANC/DANISH KRONE/DEUTSCHMARK/ FRENCH FRANC/IRISH PUNT/LUX FRANC/ DUTCH GUILDER:	$2\frac{1}{4}$% BAND.
	ITALIAN LIRA	6% band
Sept 1979	Deutschmark	+ 2.0%
	Danish krone	− 2.9%
Nov 1979	Danish krone	− 4.8%
Mar 1981	Italian lira	− 6.0%
Oct 1981	Deutschmark/Dutch guilder	+ 5.5%
	Italian lira/French franc	− 3%
Feb 1982	Danish krone	− 3.0%
	Belgian franc	− 8.5%
Jun 1982	Deutschmark/Dutch guilder	+ 4.25%
	Italian lira	− 2.75%
	French franc	− 5.75%
Mar 1983	Deutschmark	+ 5.5%
	Dutch guilder	+ 3.5%
	Danish krone	+ 2.5%
	Belgian franc	+ 1.5%

	French franc/Italian lira	− 2.5%
	Irish punt	− 3.5%
Jul 1985	All except Italy	+ 2%
	Italy	− 6%
Apr 1986	Deutschmark/Dutch guilder	+ 3%
	Belgian franc/Danish krone	+ 1%
	French franc	− 3%
Aug 1986	Irish punt	− 8%
Jan 1987	Deutschmark/Dutch guilder	+ 3%
	Belgian franc	+ 2%
July 1989	SPANISH PESETA JOINS	6% band
Jan 1990	Italian lira	− 3.7%
	LIRA BAND NOW 2¼%	
Oct 1990	BRITISH POUND JOINS	6% band

Note that all EC currencies are included in the ECU's value.

GUIDE TO FURTHER READING

•••

The most extensive analysis of the costs and benefits of introducing a single European currency was sponsored by the European Commission. The results were forwarded to the European Council in August 1990, and have subsequently been published in a variety of forms. The most amenable of these for the non-specialist reader is:
The ECU Report by Michael Emerson and Christopher Huhne (Pan, 1991) with an introduction by Jacques Delors.

A more technical guide to the economics of monetary union appears in:
Achieving Monetary Union in Europe by Andrew Britton and David Mayes (Sage, 1992). This book is published with the Association for the Monetary Union of Europe. Not too surprisingly, given their sponsors, both books conclude that a single currency area is a good thing. They focus on the advantages of an exchange rate target for policy discipline and the ultimate transactions savings from pan-European use of the ECU.

The economic pressures which arise from an attempt to prevent exchange rate adjustments are outlined in:
Sterling in Danger: The Economic Consequences of Pegged Exchange Rates by Alan Walters (Fontana Collins, 1990). Despite its title, the Walters book raises issue of general applicability within the ERM, not just the United Kingdom.
Books presenting both sides of the argument in a balanced way are few and far-between. That is why *The ERM Explained* was written.

For the investor and financial market practitioner interested in the ECU's current role in the financial markets, the best single guide is:
ECU: The Currency of Europe edited by Christopher Johnson (Euromoney Books, 1991). The book begins with an introduction by Jacques Delors, but its main focus is on the what and

how — not the whether. Among other issues, it gives an account of the rapid growth of the ECU in bond and money markets.

A more detailed and rigorous assessment of the performance of the EMS as a problem in financial economics is presented by: *Limiting Exchange Rate Flexibility: The European Monetary System* by Francesco Giavazzi & Alberto Giovannini (The MIT Press, 1989). Mathematical models are used in an attempt to assess technical problems of the EMS's operation such as 'dollar-DMark polarization'.

For some readers, the contents of this book will have whetted their appetite for understanding economic issues. Many of these are fundamentally straightforward but are made impenetrable by the jargon:
The Economist: Economics by Rupert Pennant-Rea and Clive Crook (Penguin, 1986) explains the disputes which divide monetarist and Keynesian approaches to economic management.

For others, at a time of rapid institutional change in Europe, there may be strong business reasons to keep well-informed of current development. Among a series of excellent publications from the EIU:
The Economist Intelligence Unit: European Trends (Business International Limited) is a journal providing regular updates on the European scene.

Finally, among publications describing the practical opportunities offered by reduced barriers to trade:
1992: Strategies for the Single Market by James Dudley (Kogan Page, 1990). The devaluations of sterling and the lira provide an extra incentive for businesses in the UK and Italy to seek out profitable export opportunities in the new European Economic Area.

Index